Real World Colouring Book

For Advanced Users & Adults

50 Images

Created From Real Life Photos For You To Colour As You Please.

ISBN 978-0-359-86340-2
90000
9 780359 863402

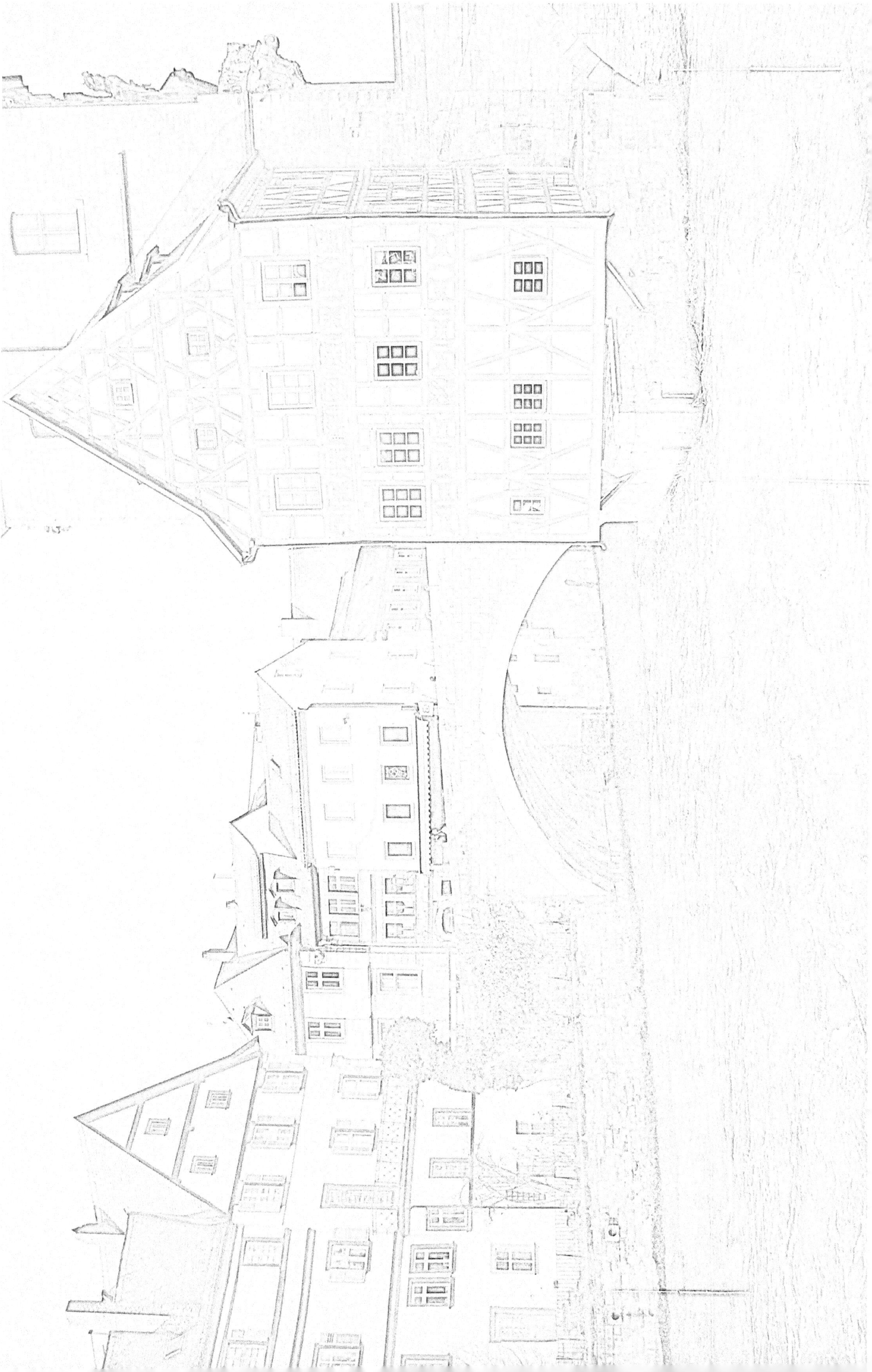

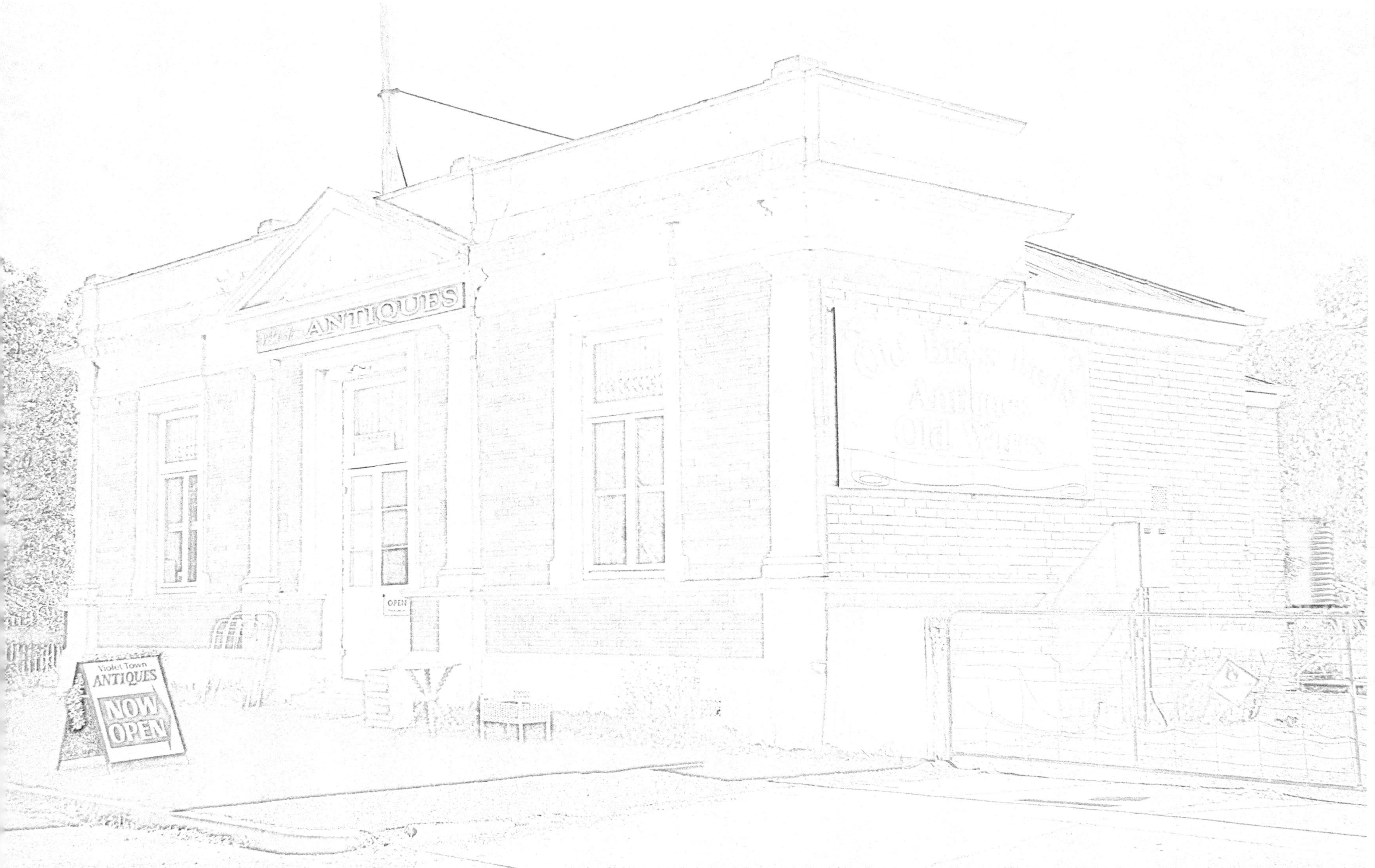
ANTIQUES
OPEN
Violet Town
ANTIQUES
NOW
OPEN

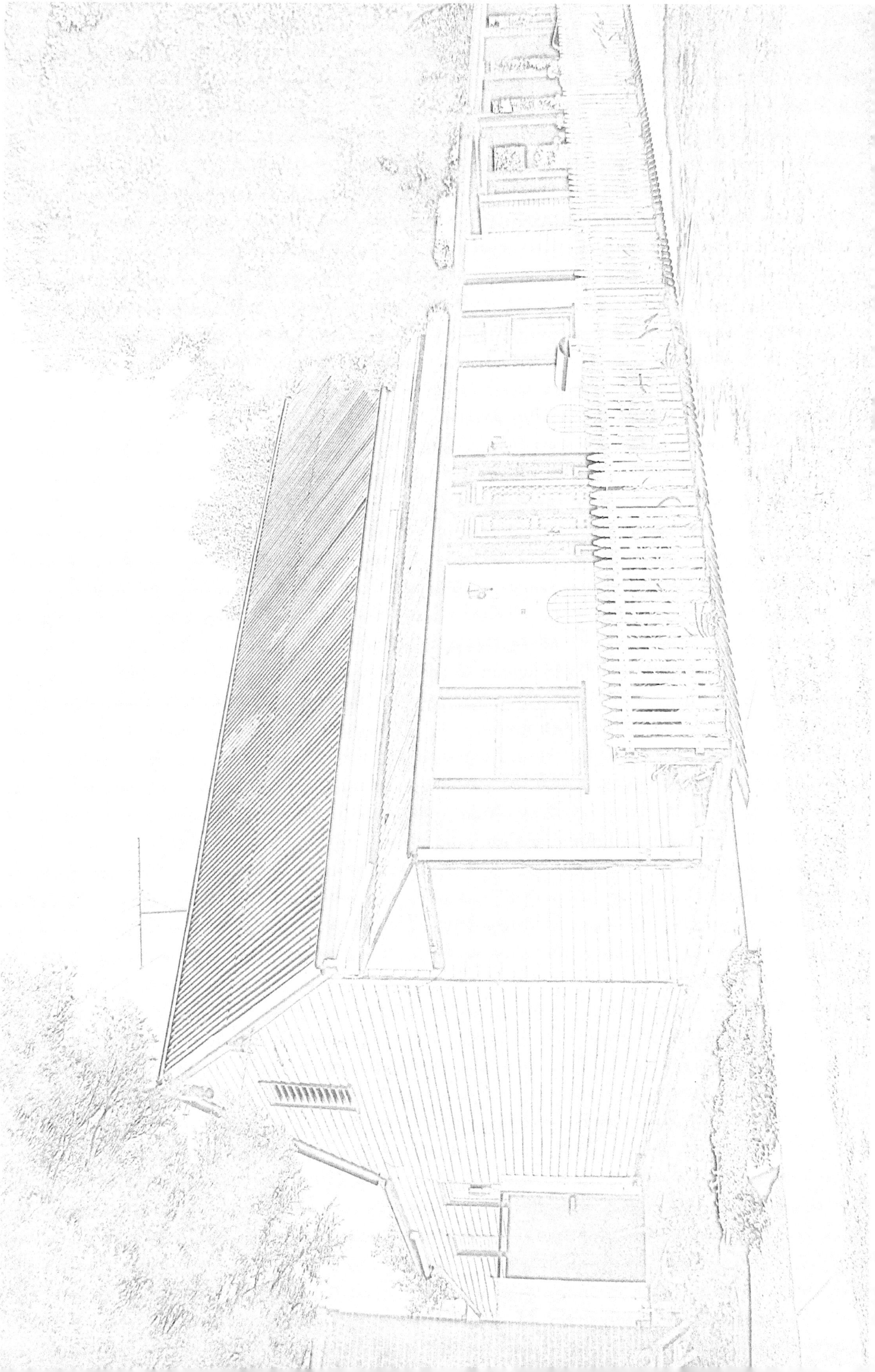

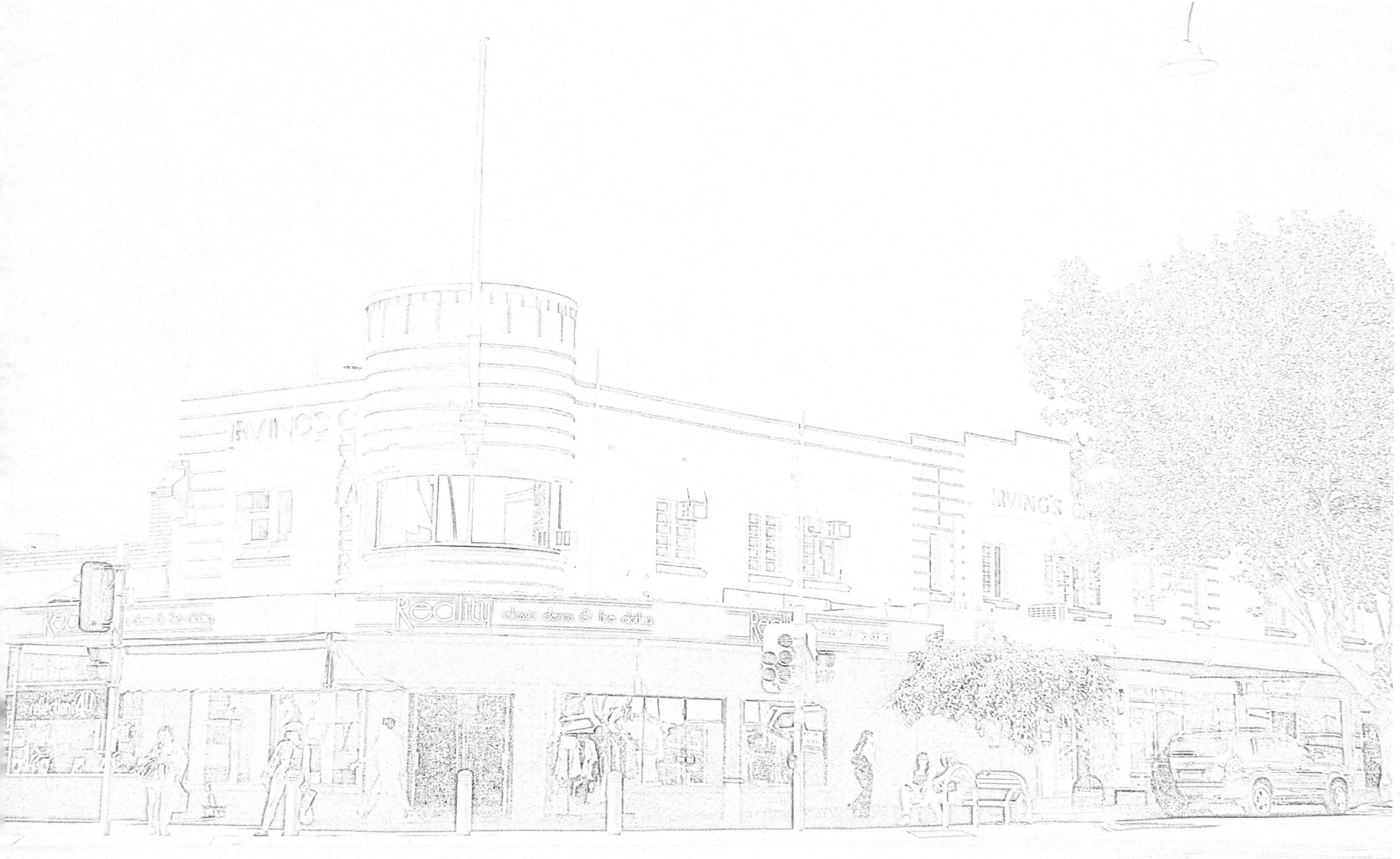
IRVING'S
Reality
classic denim & fine clothing
IRVING'S

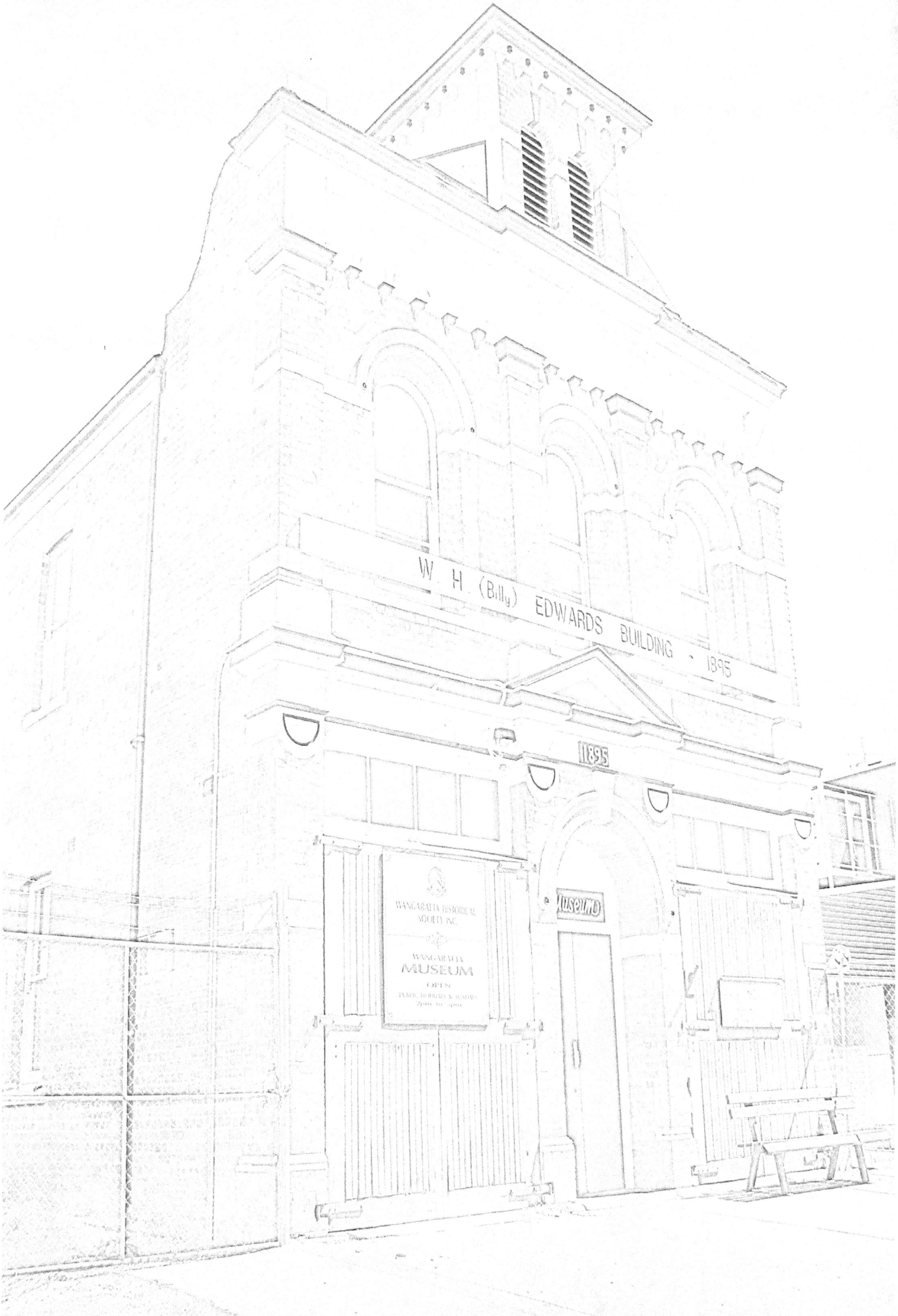
W. H. (Billy) EDWARDS BUILDING · 1895
1895
Museum
WANGARATTA HISTORICAL SOCIETY INC.
WANGARATTA
MUSEUM
OPEN

19 28
BUFFALO
BUILDING
ors
2344
Conveyancing & All Legal Services
Jabo
96

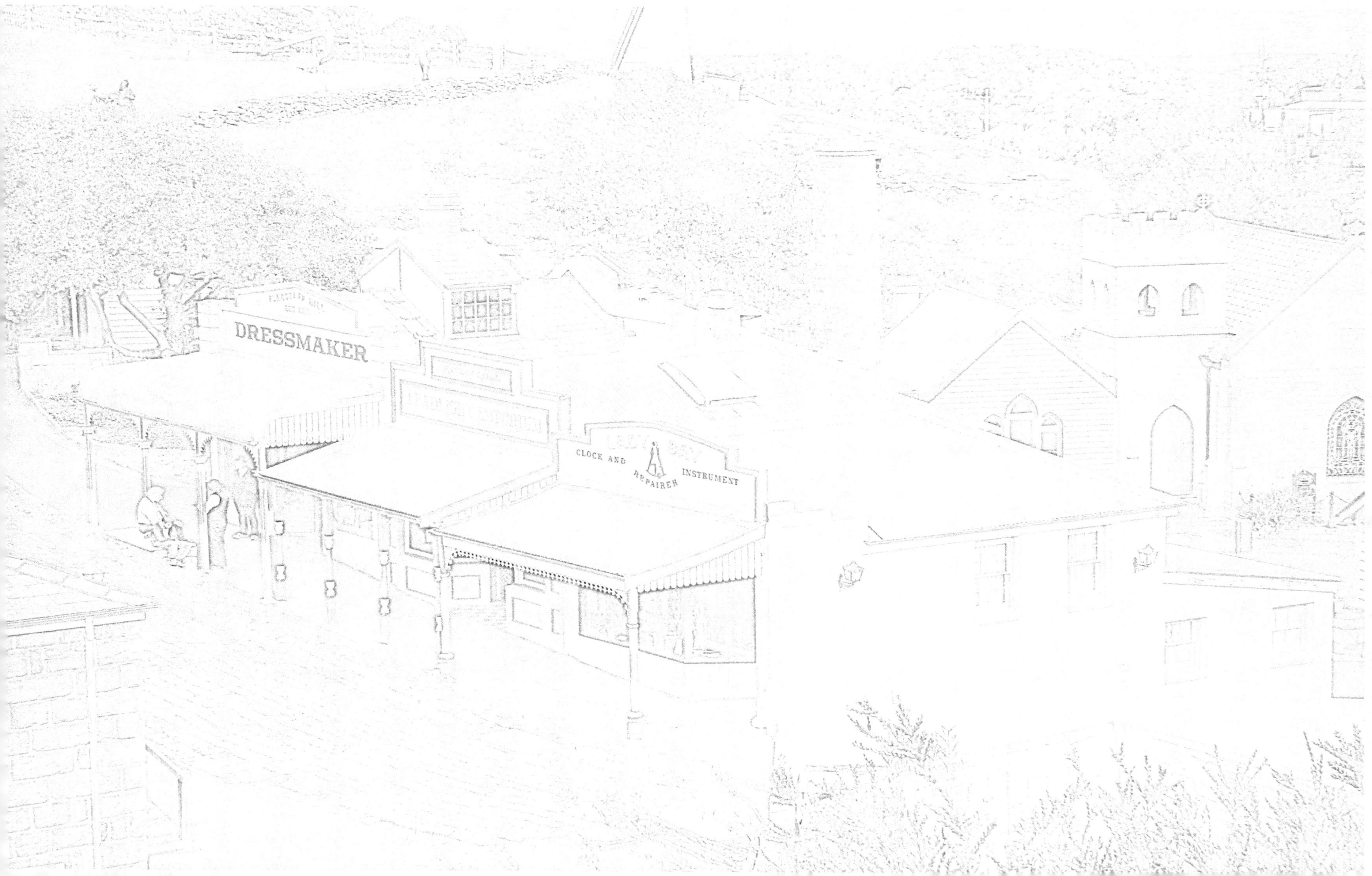
DRESSMAKER
CLOCK AND INSTRUMENT REPAIRER

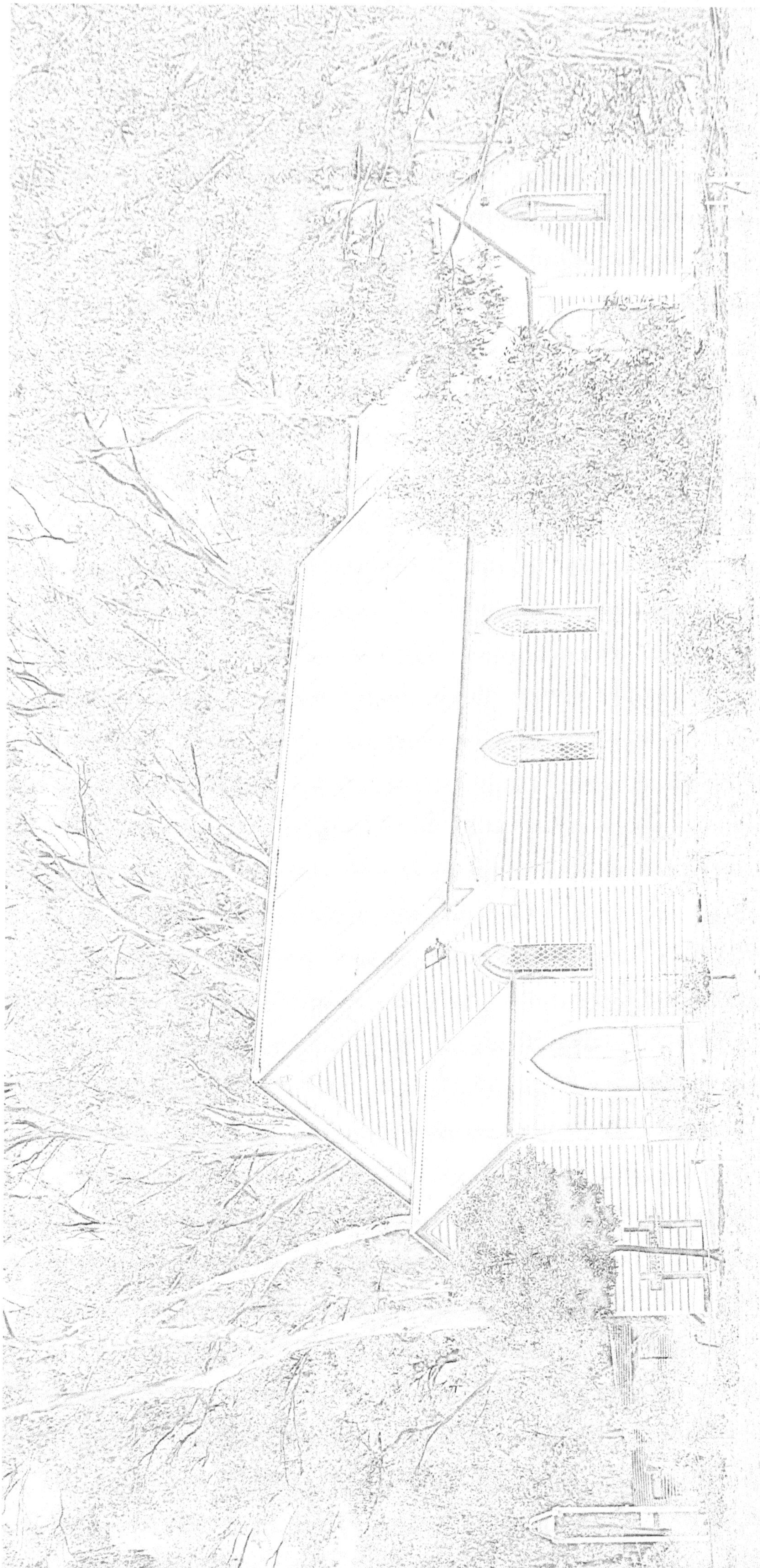

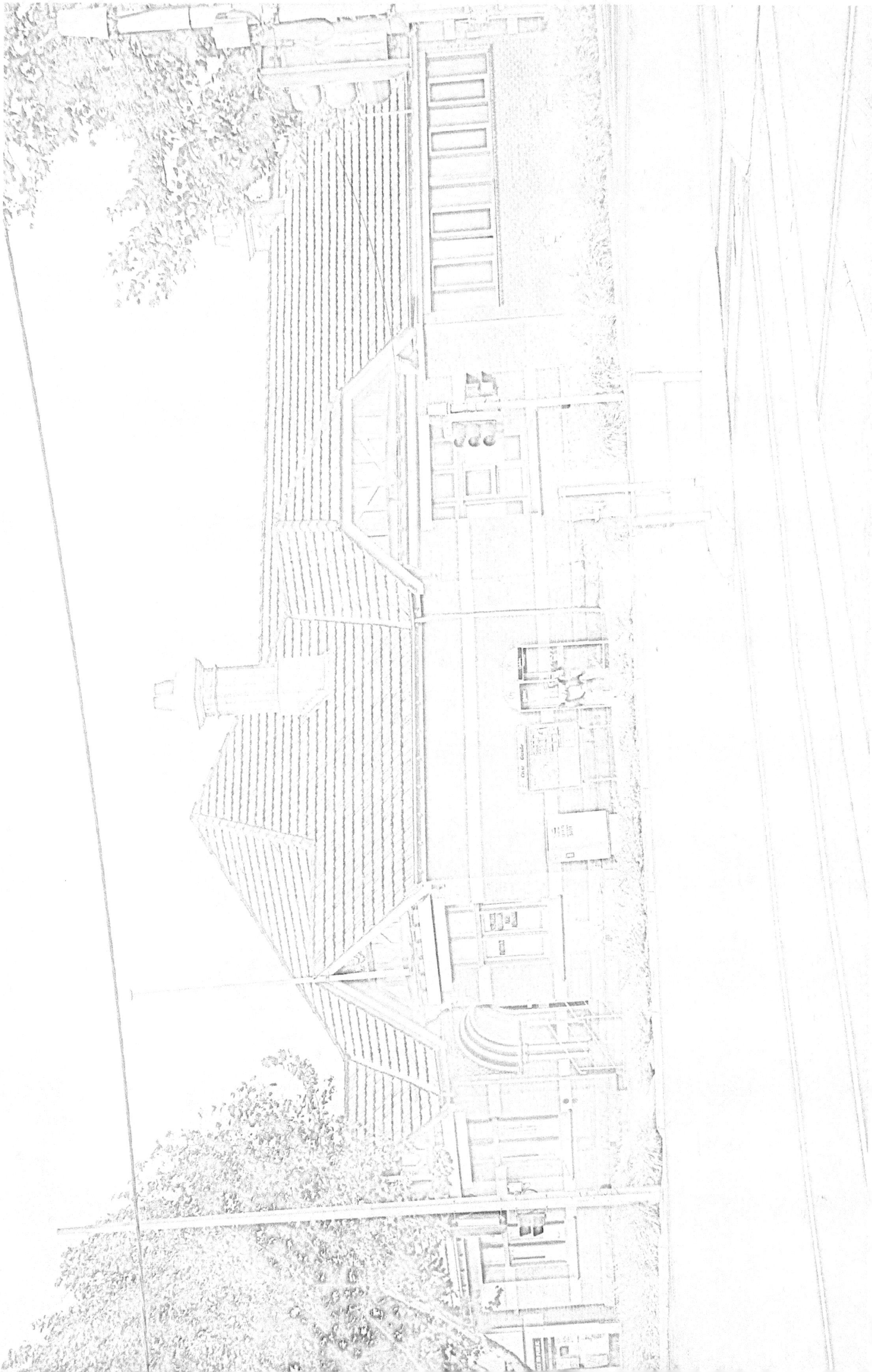

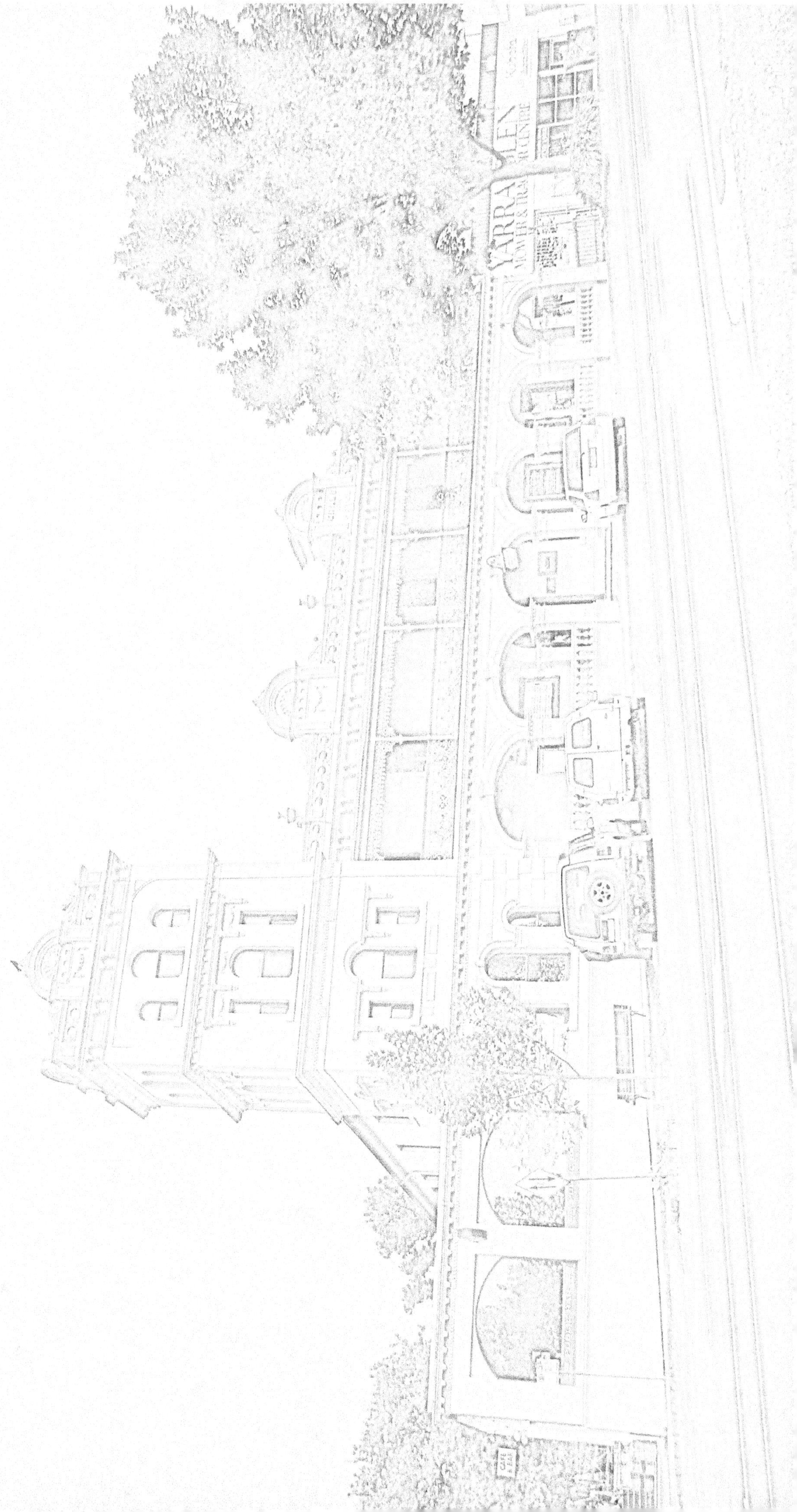

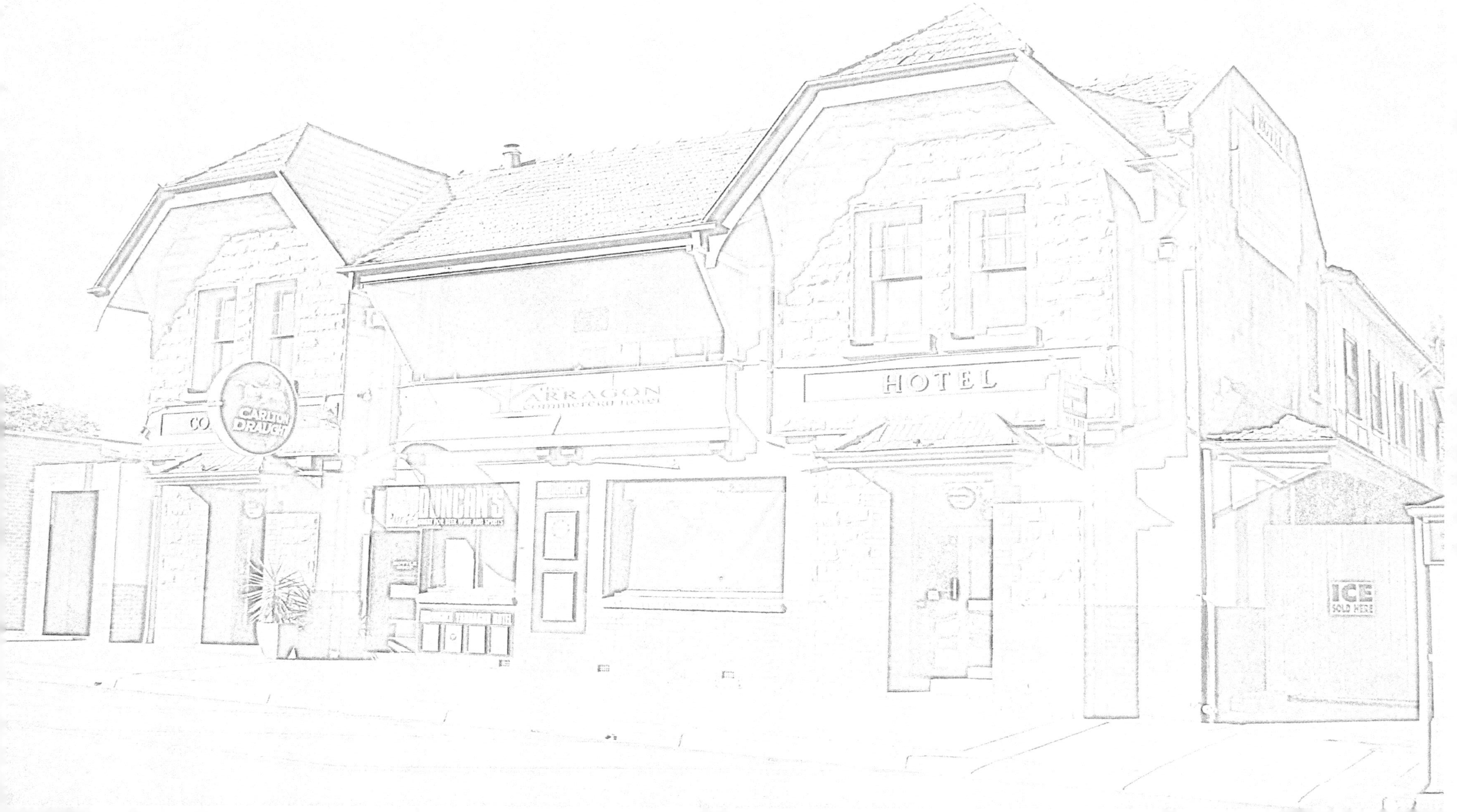
HOTEL
YARRAGON
commercial hotel
CARLTON DRAUGHT
DUNCAN'S
ICE
SOLD HERE

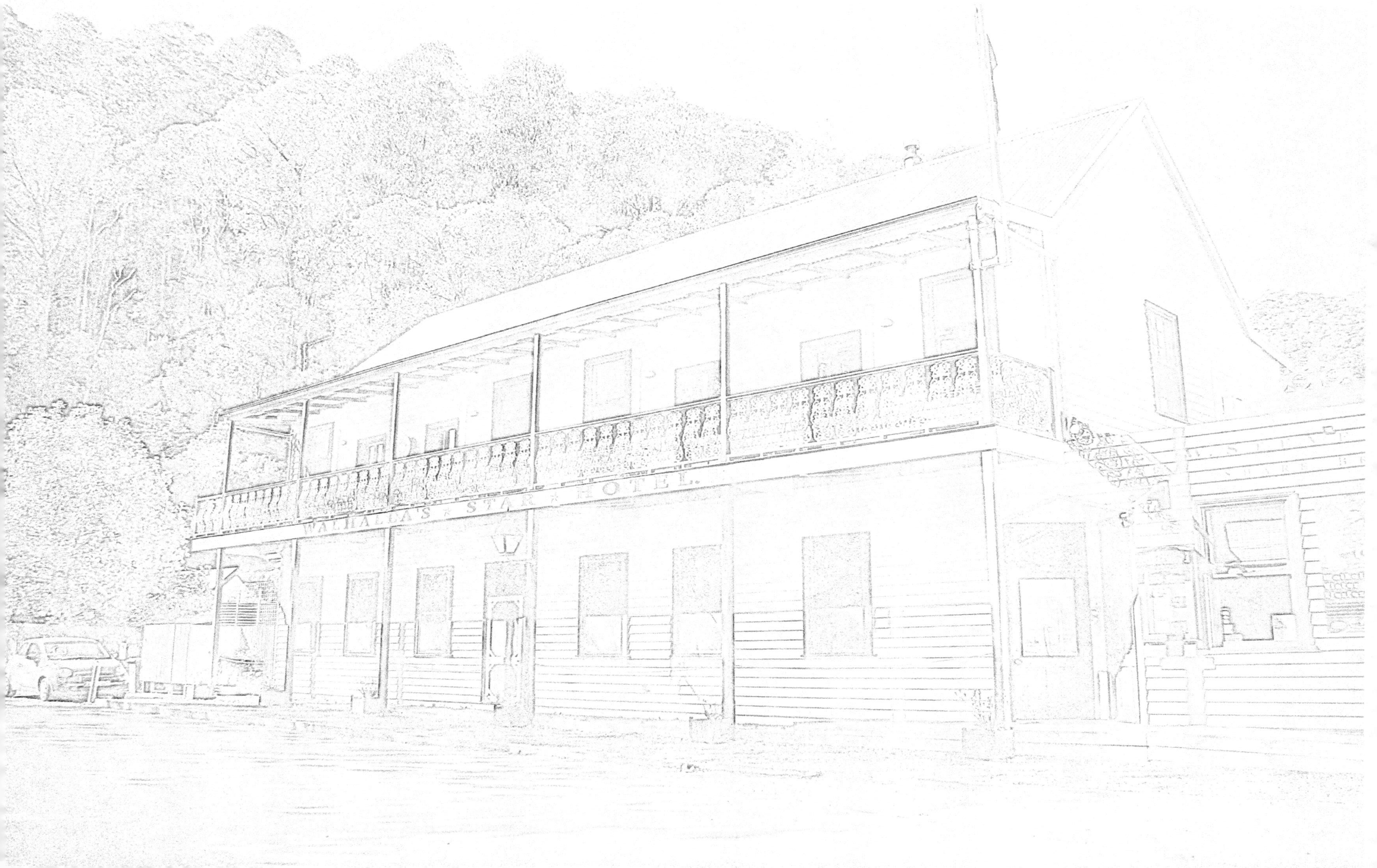
WALHALLA'S ★ STAR ★ HOTEL.

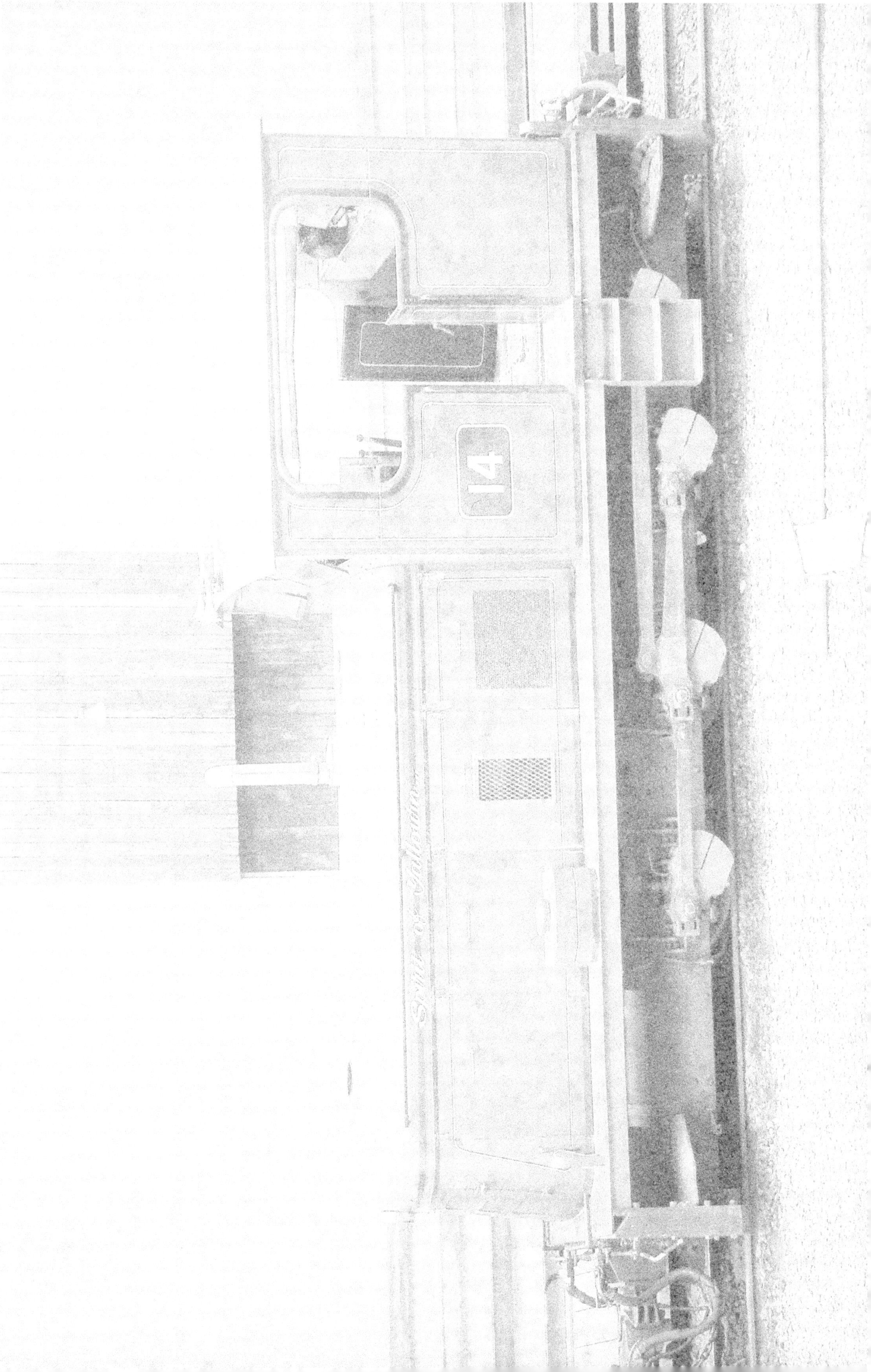
14

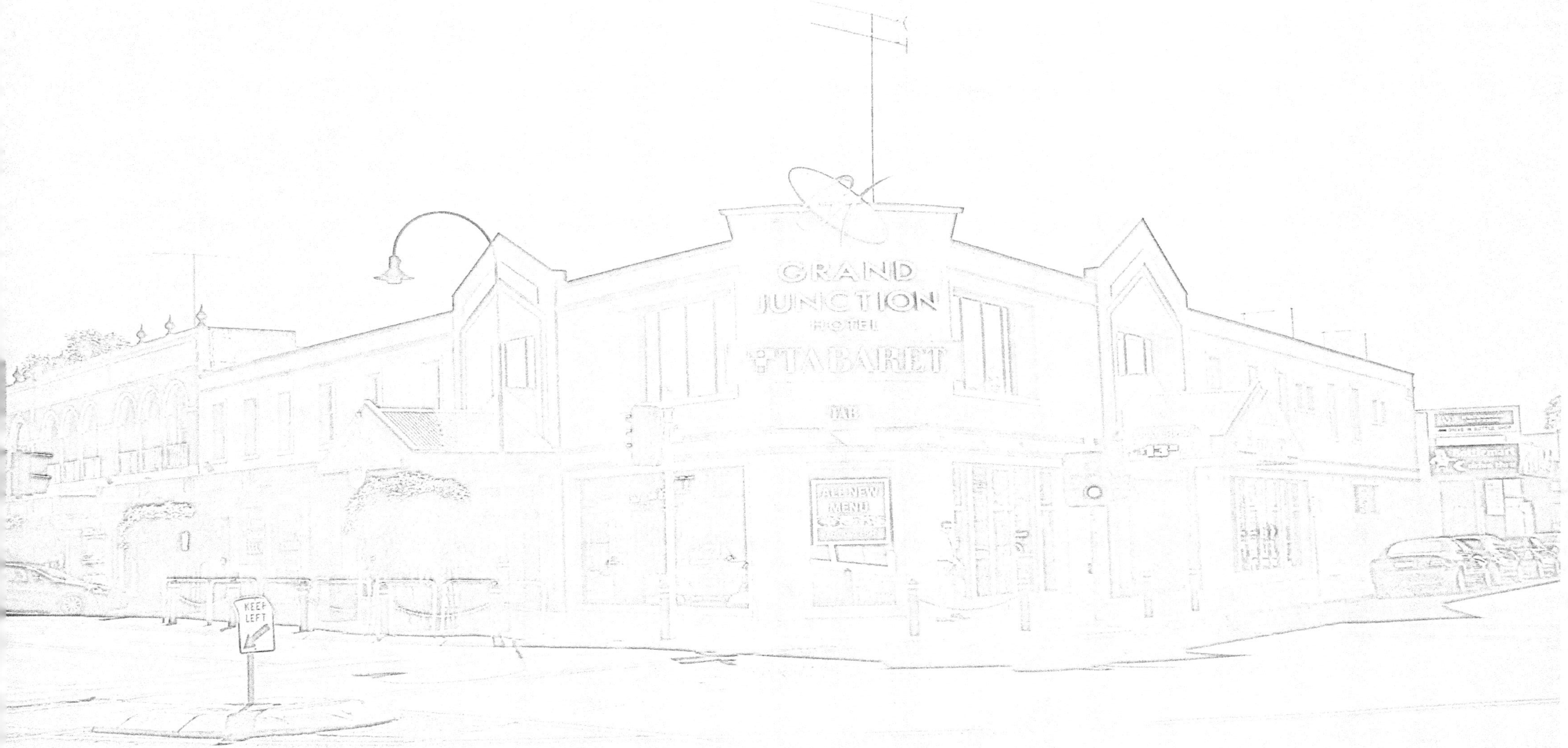
GRAND
JUNCTION
HOTEL
TAB
ALL NEW
MENU
KEEP
LEFT

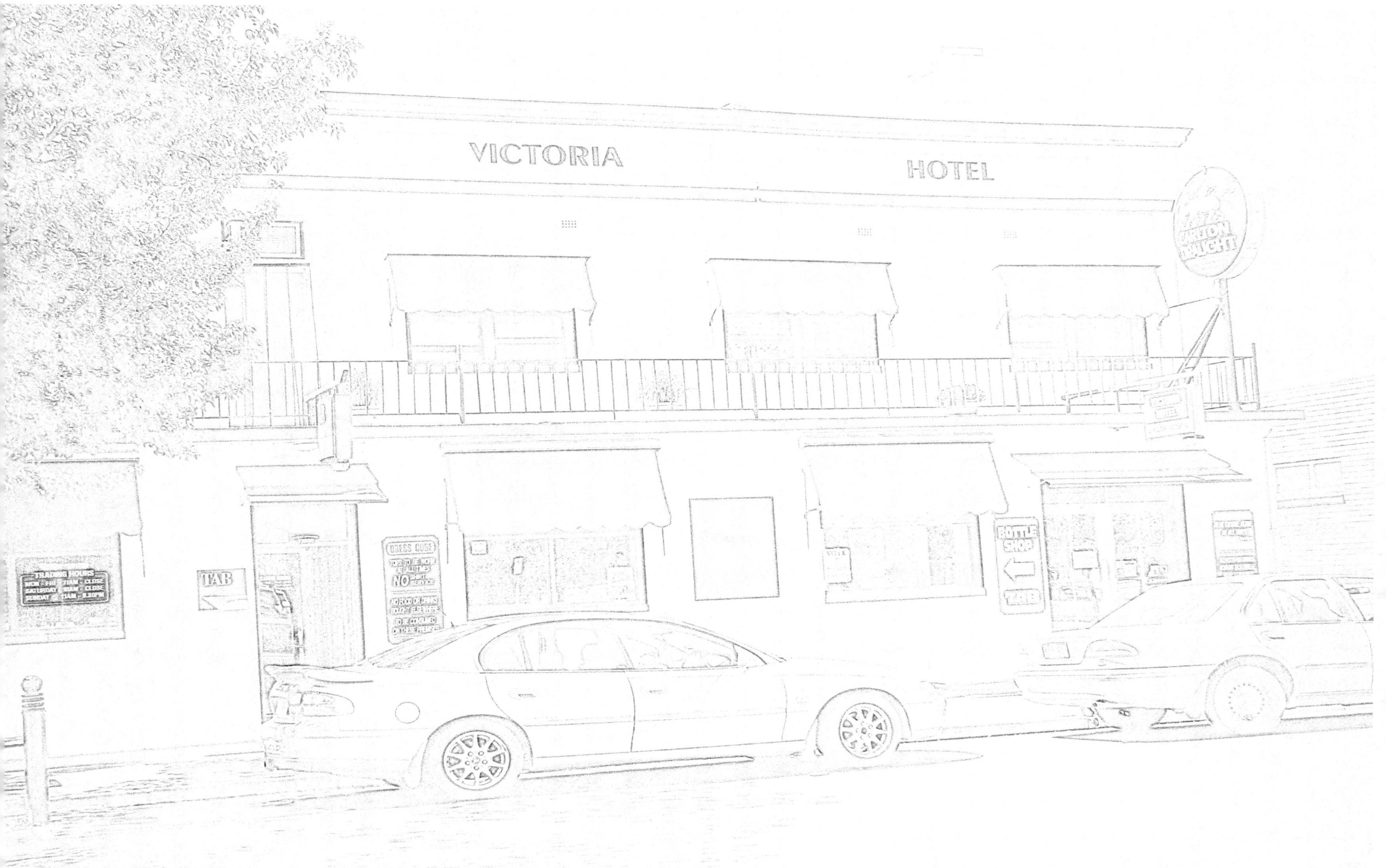
VICTORIA
HOTEL
TAB
DRESS CODE
BOTTLE SHOP
TAB

RESTAURANT

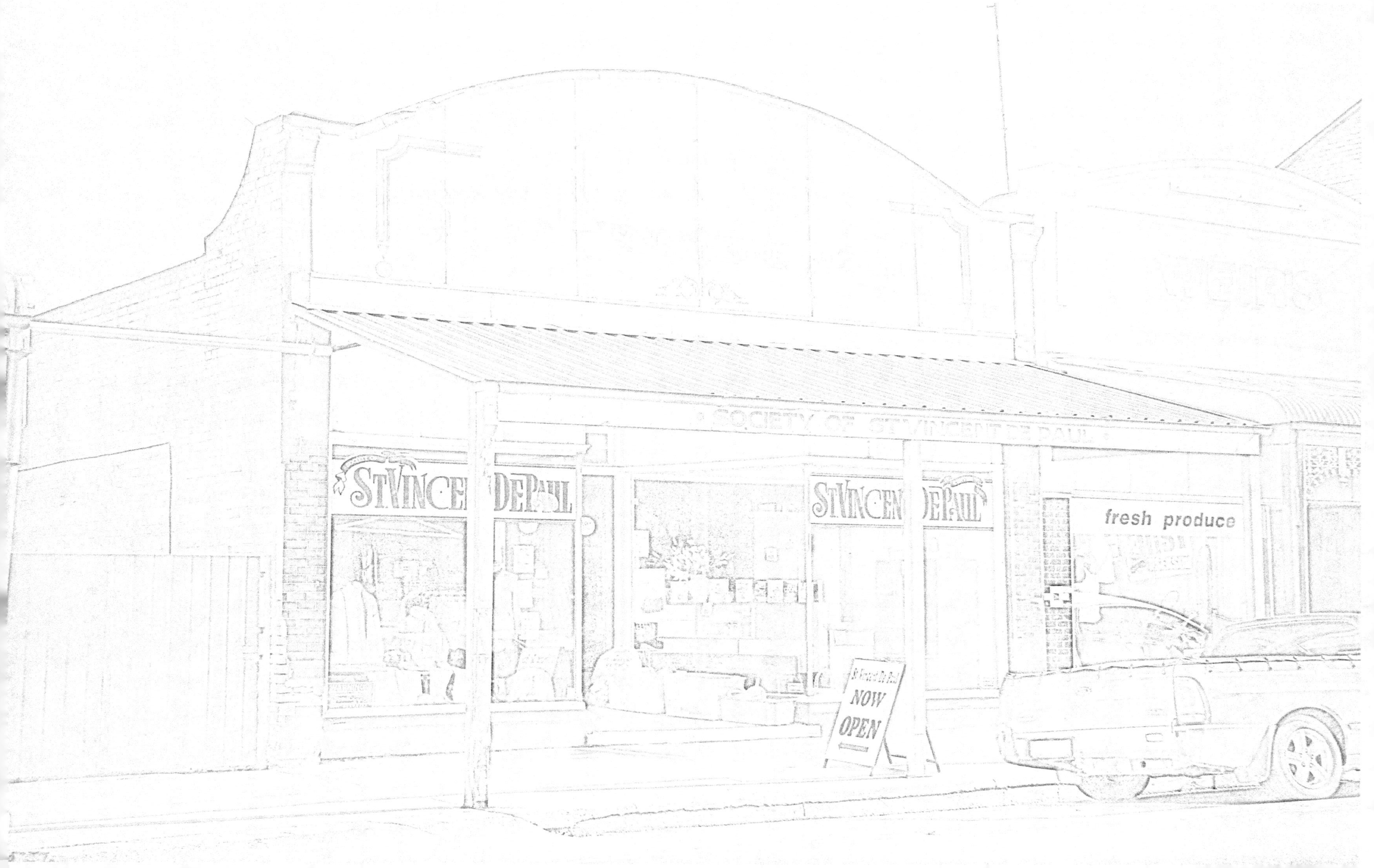
SOCIETY OF ST VINCENT DE PAUL
St Vincent De Paul
St Vincent De Paul
fresh produce
NOW
OPEN

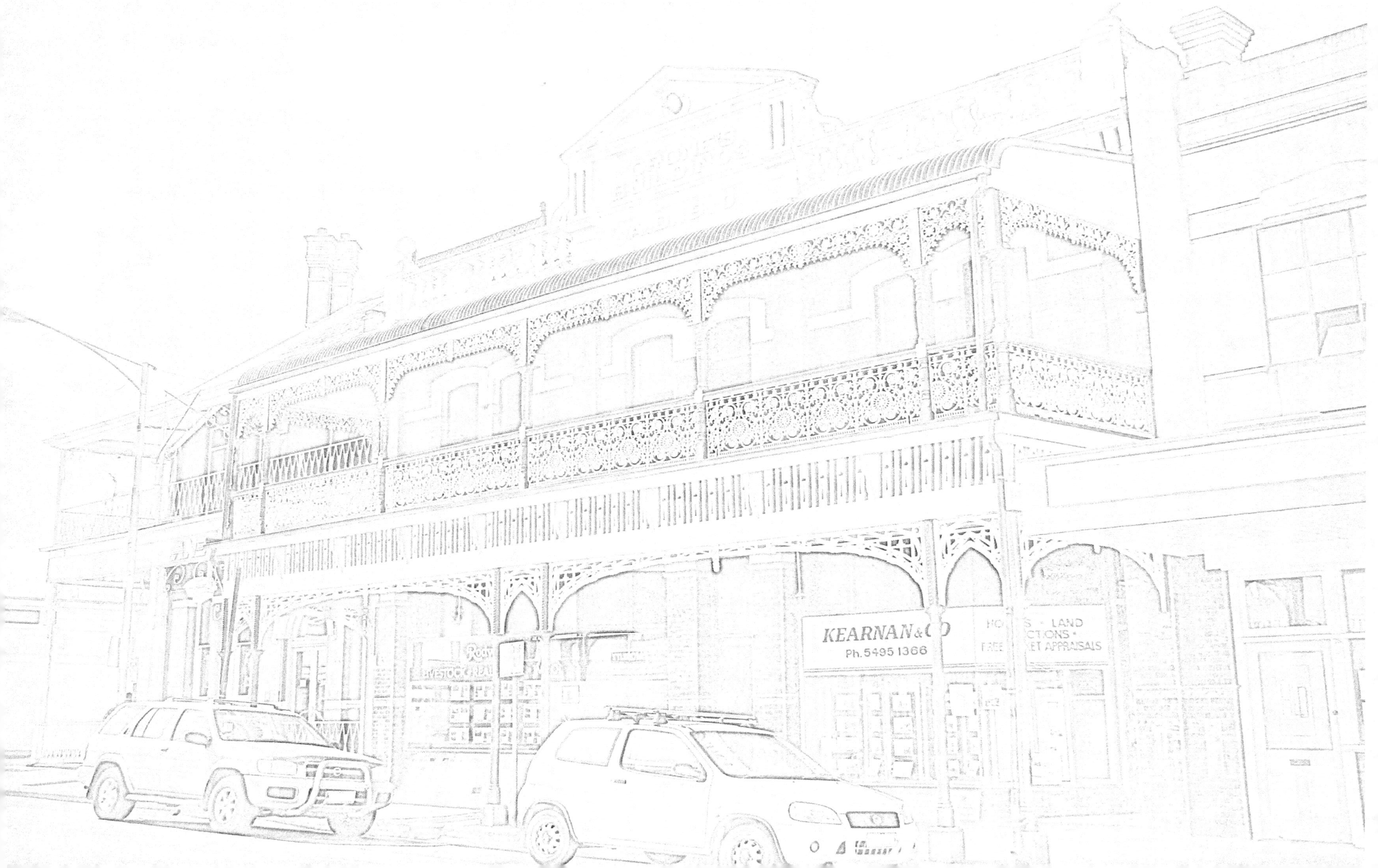
KEARNAN & CO
Ph. 5495 1366

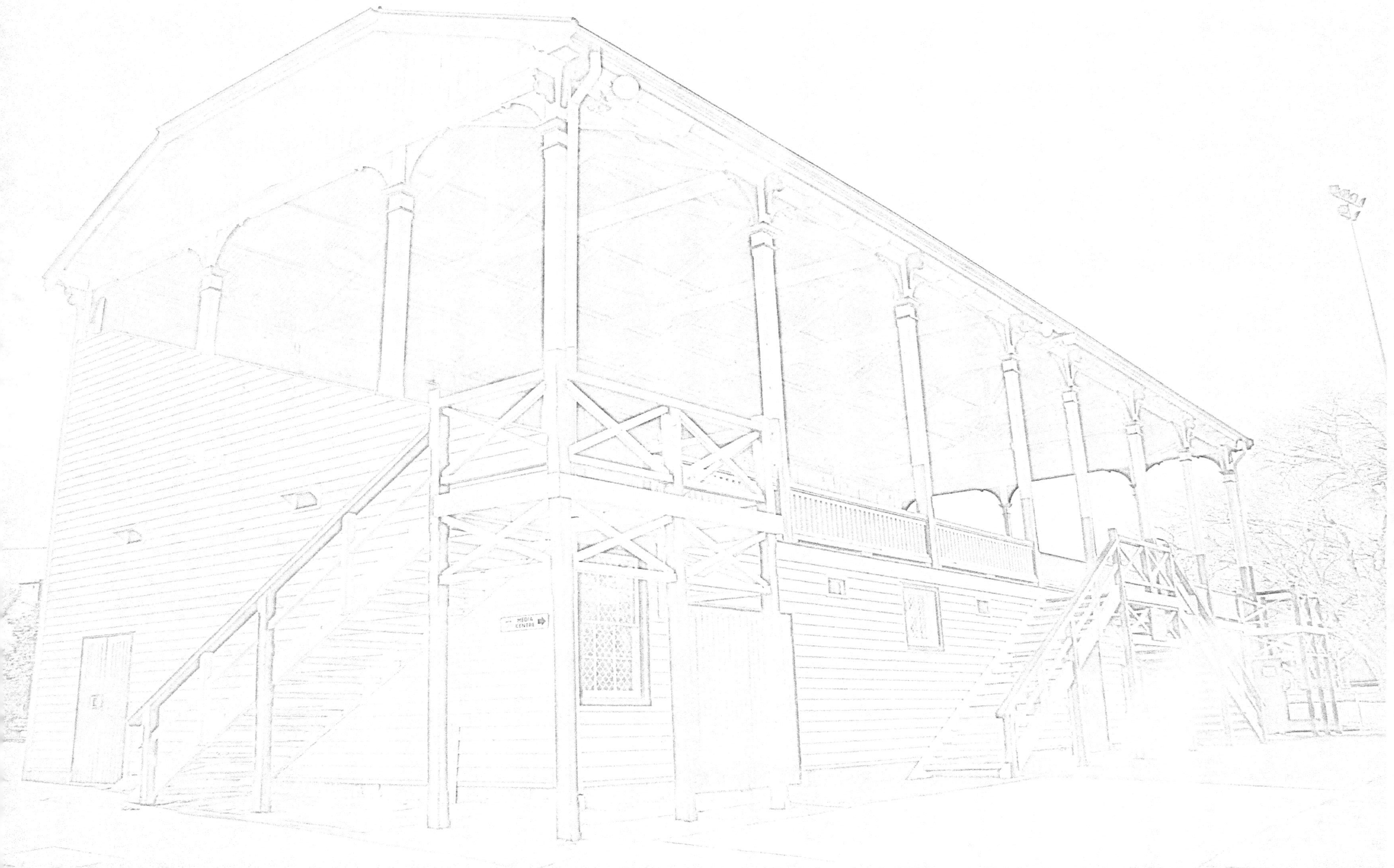
MEDIA CENTRE

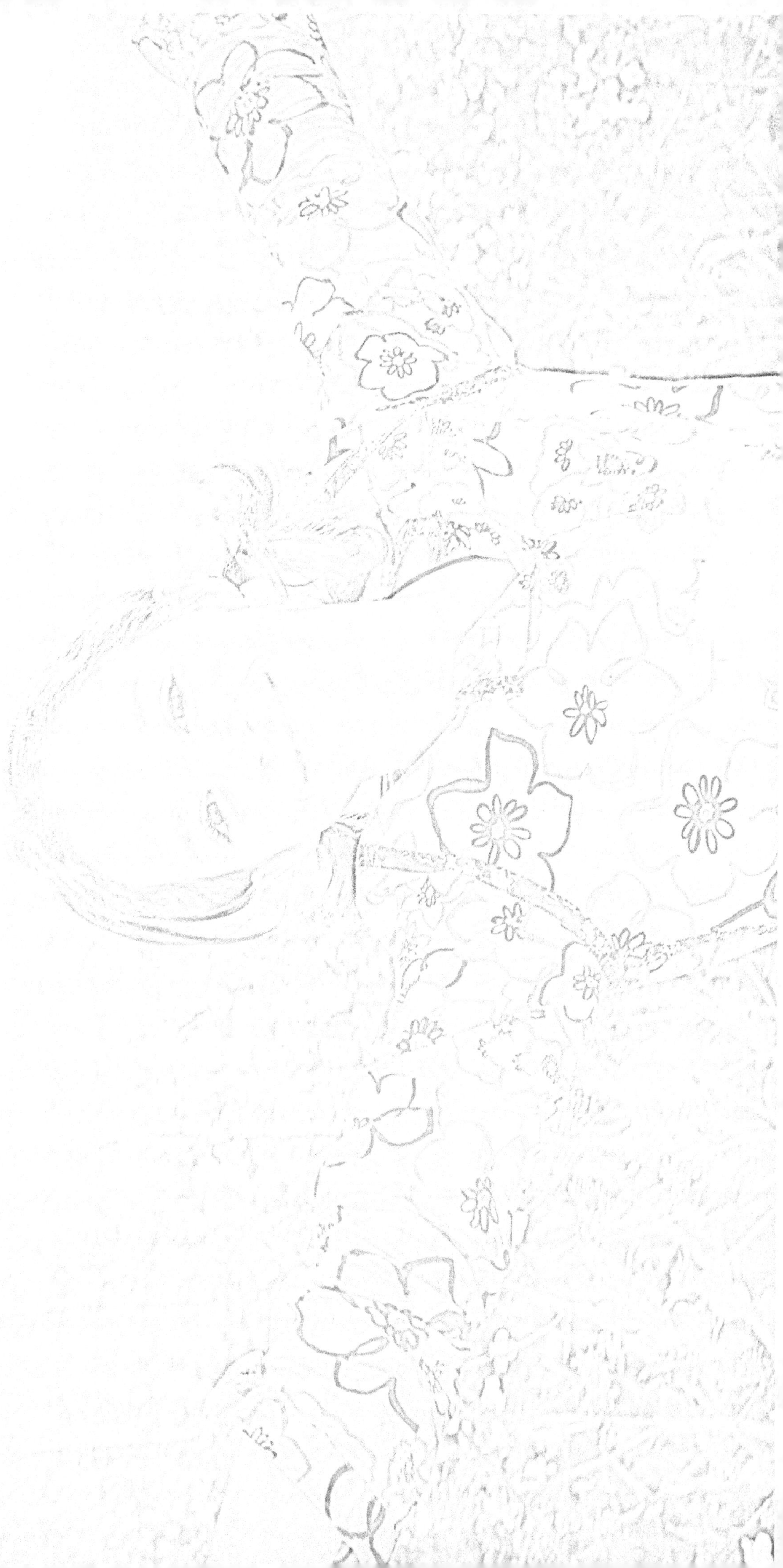

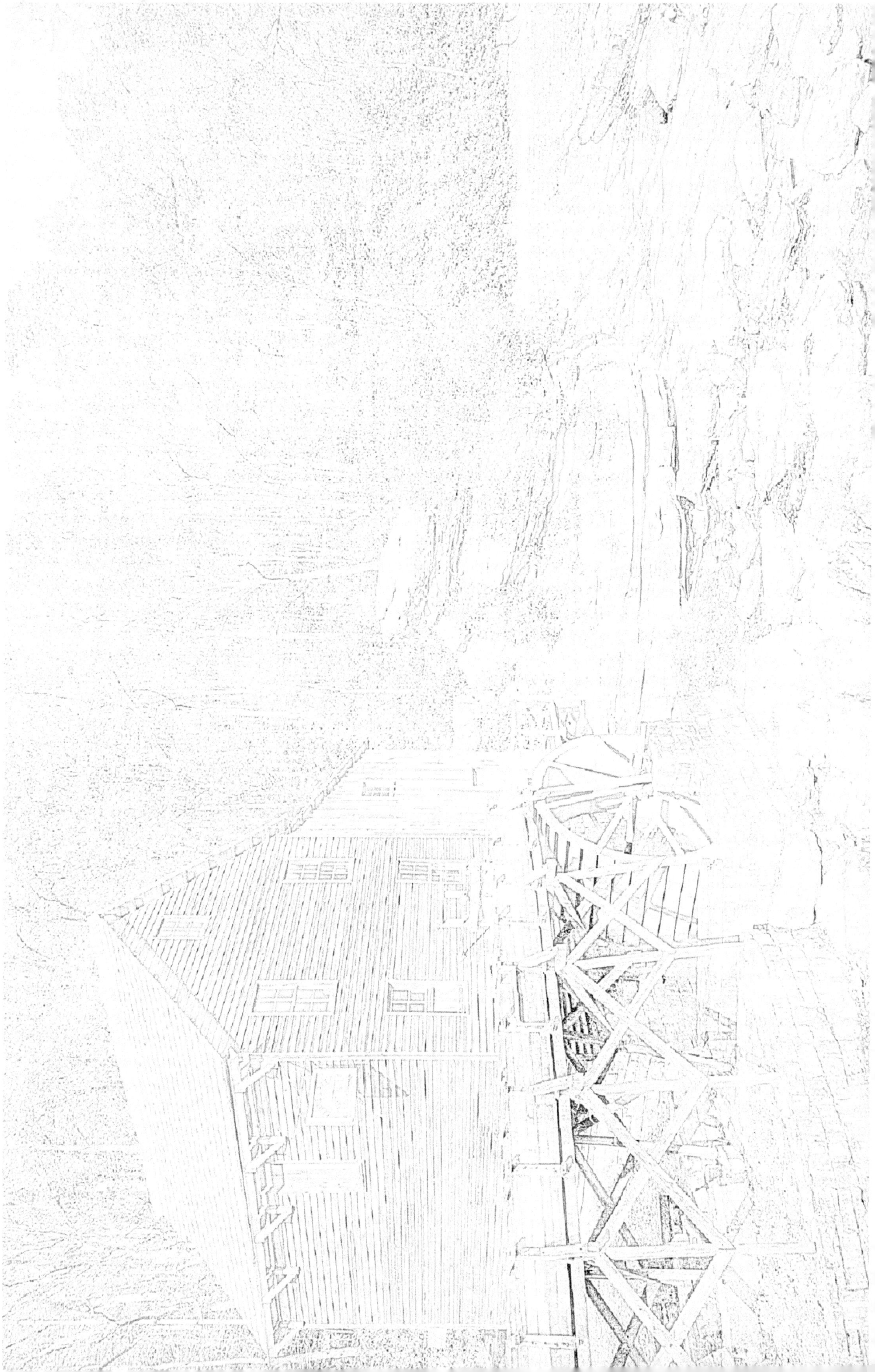

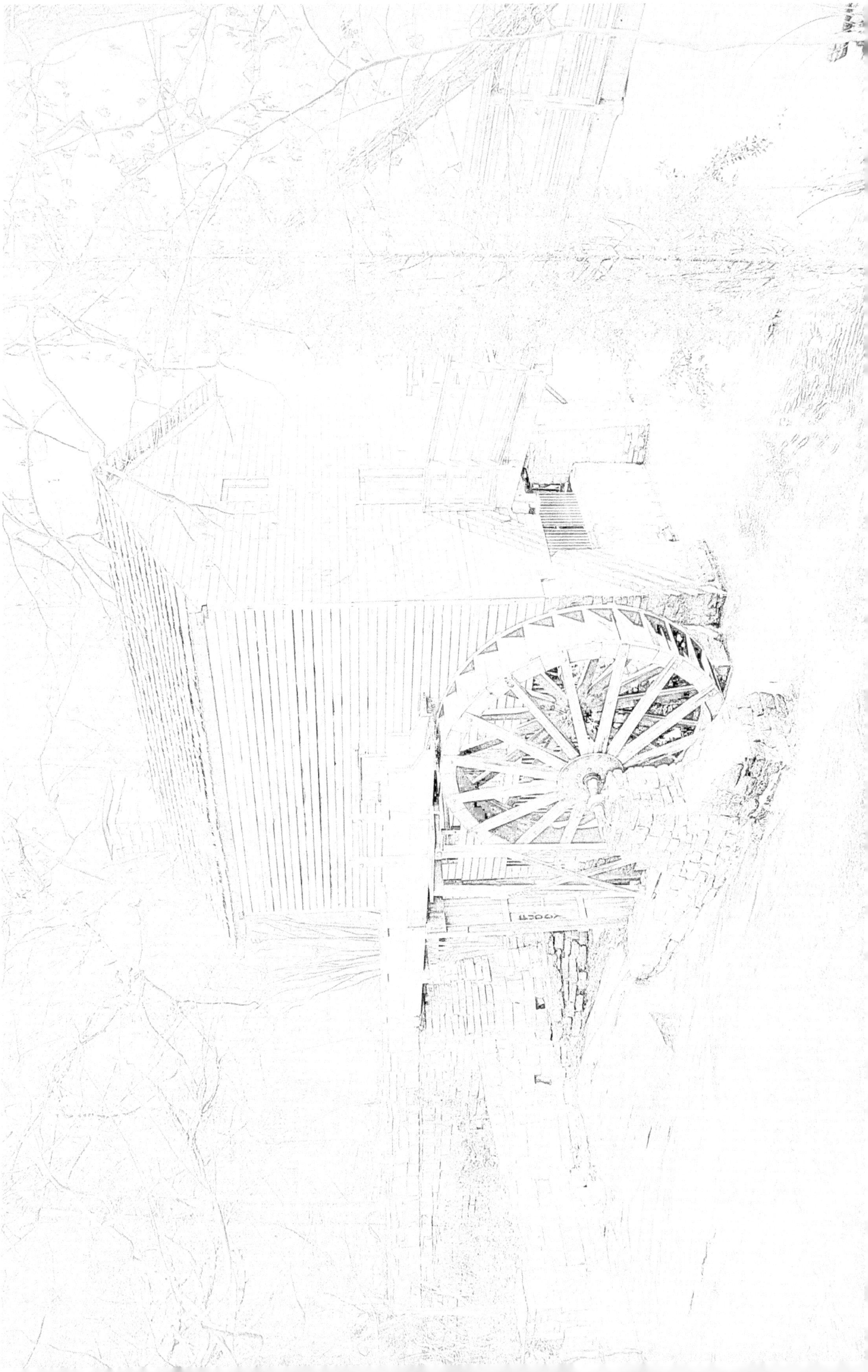

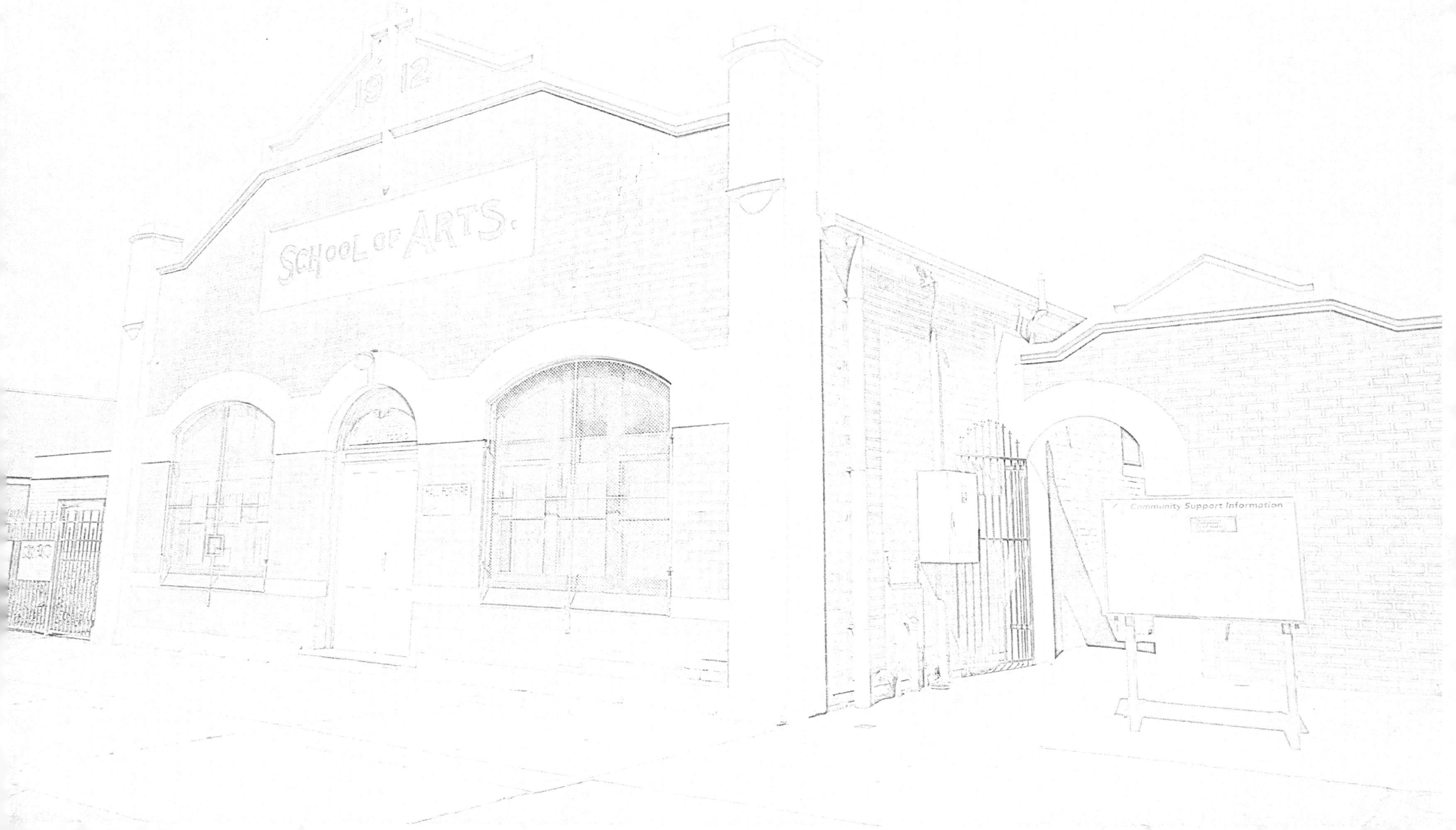
1912
SCHOOL OF ARTS.
Community Support Information

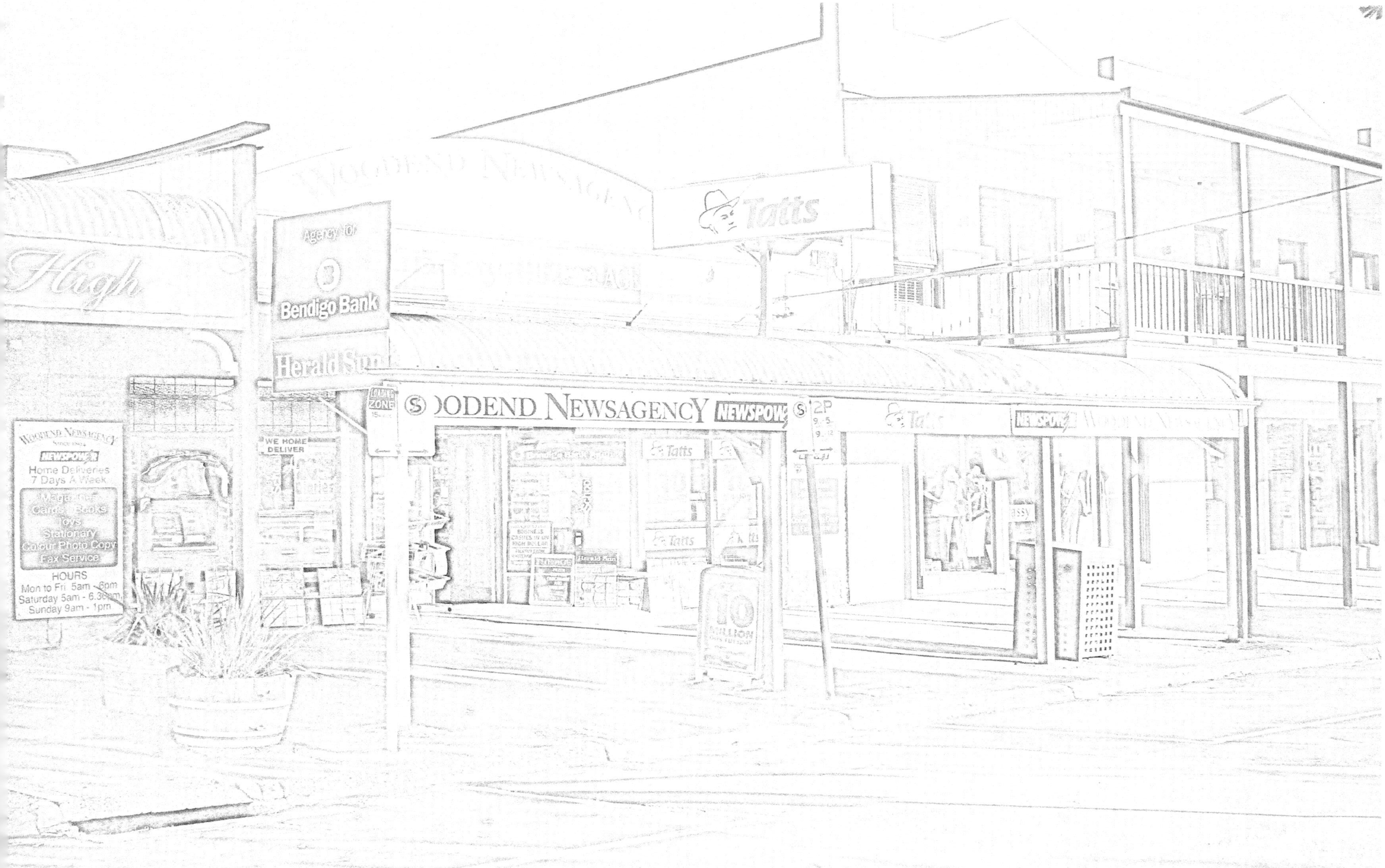
High
Agency for
Bendigo Bank
Herald Sun
Tatts
OODEND NEWSAGENCY
NEWSPOWER
WE HOME DELIVER
Woodend Newsagency
NEWSPOWER
Home Deliveries
7 Days A Week
Magazines
Cards Books
Toys
Stationary
Colour Photo Copy
Fax Service
HOURS
Mon to Fri 5am - 6pm
Saturday 5am - 6.30pm
Sunday 9am - 1pm
2P
LOADING ZONE
10 MILLION

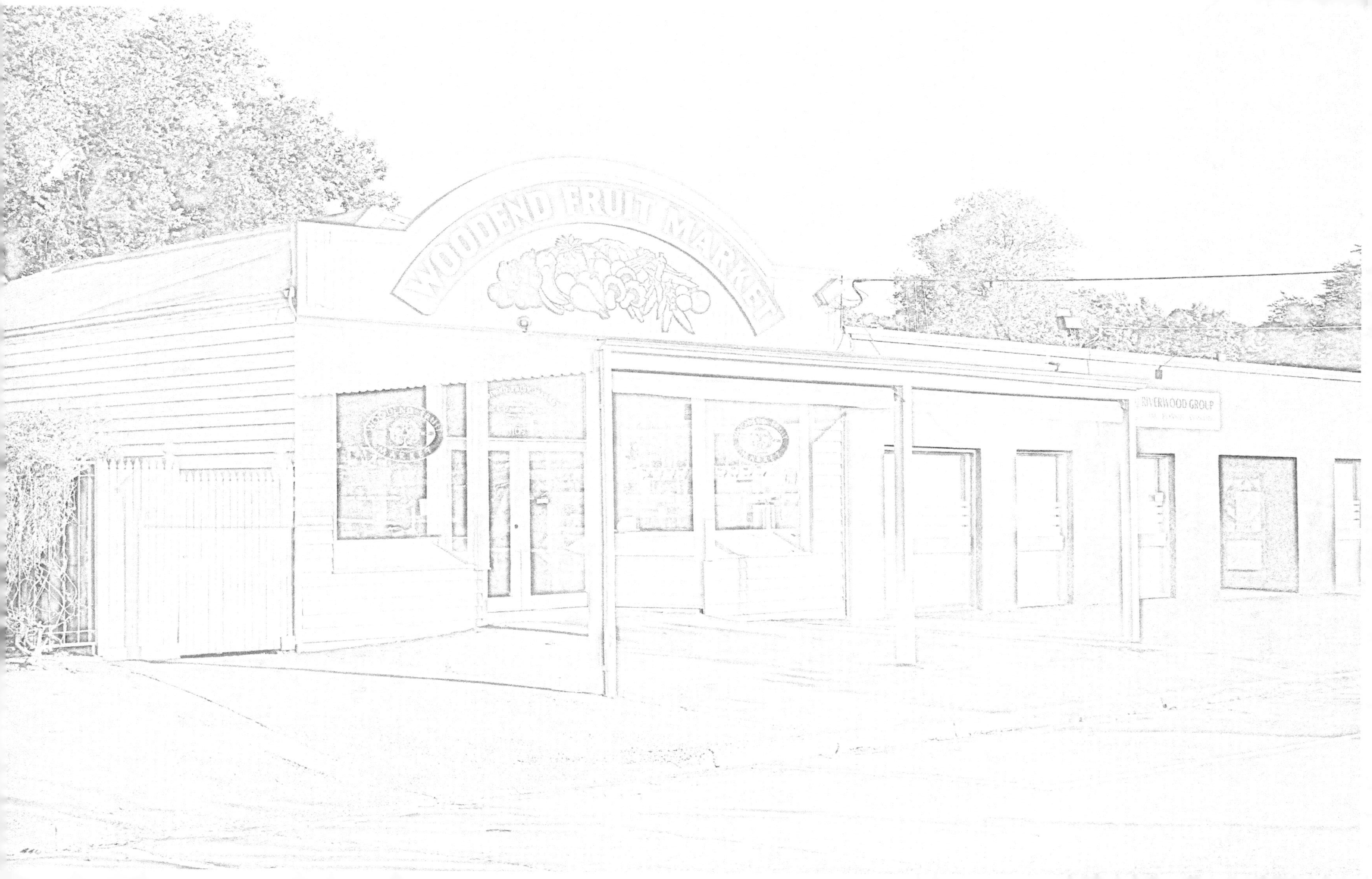
WOODEND FRUIT MARKET
RIVERWOOD GROUP

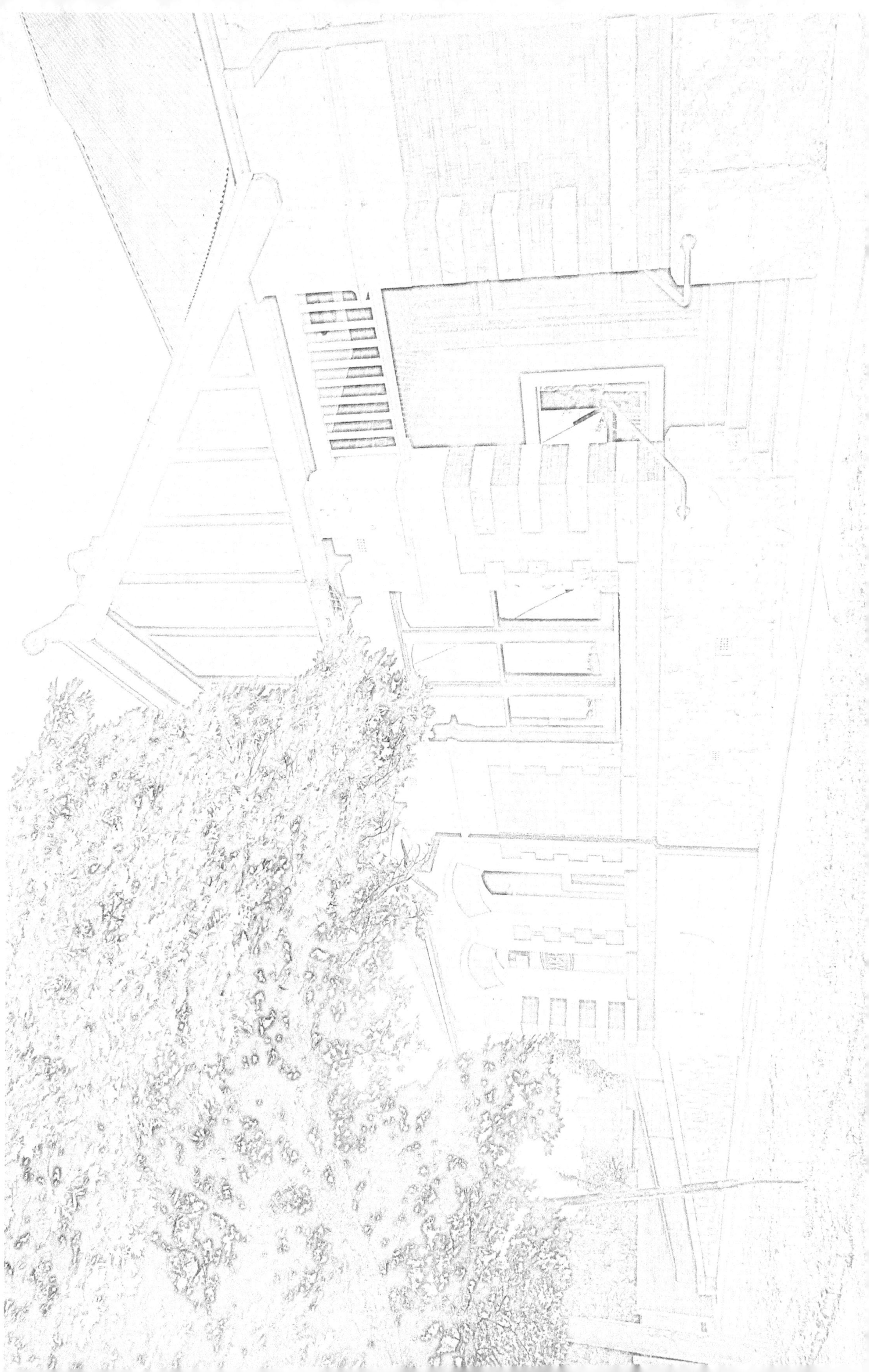

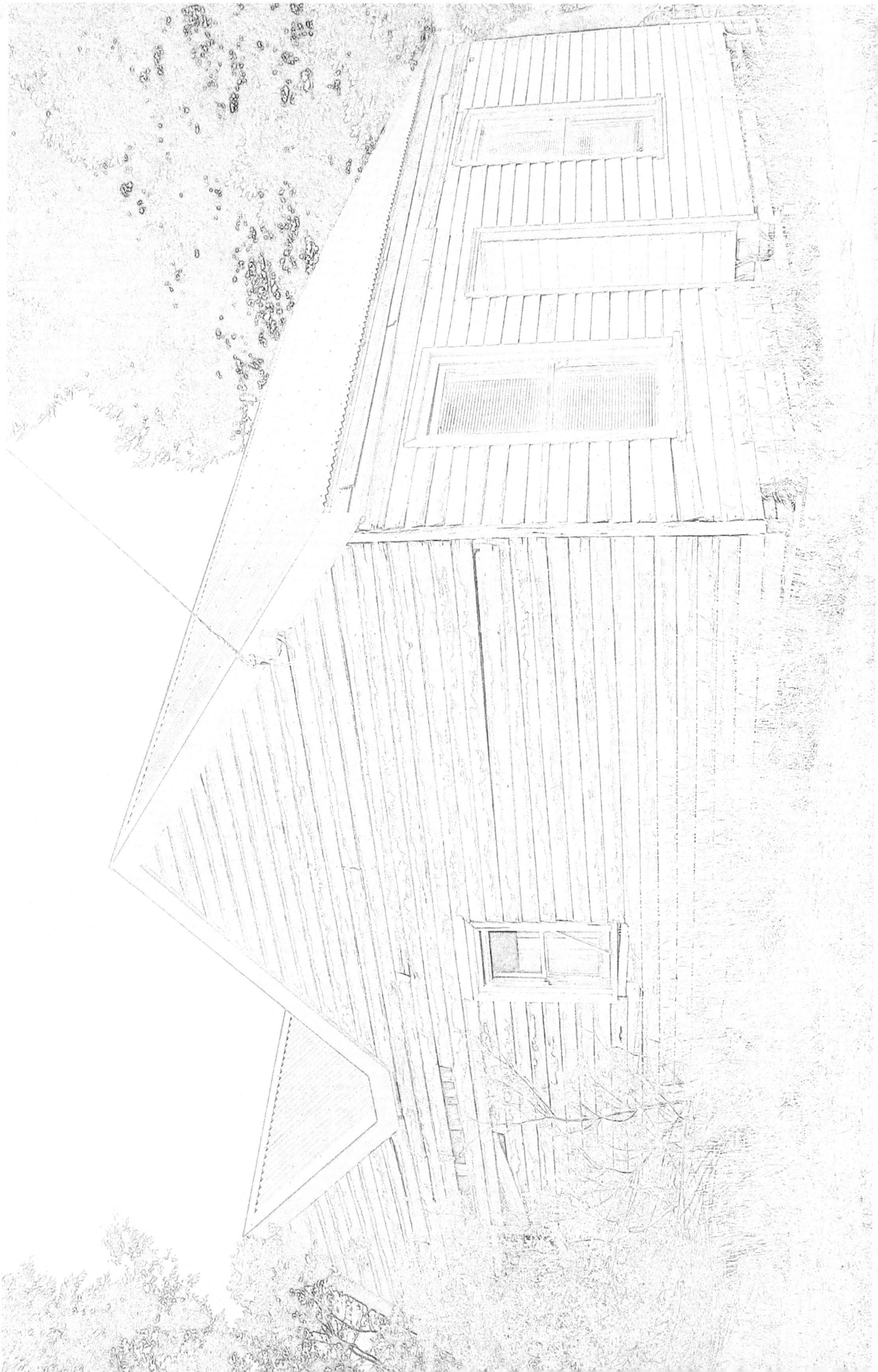

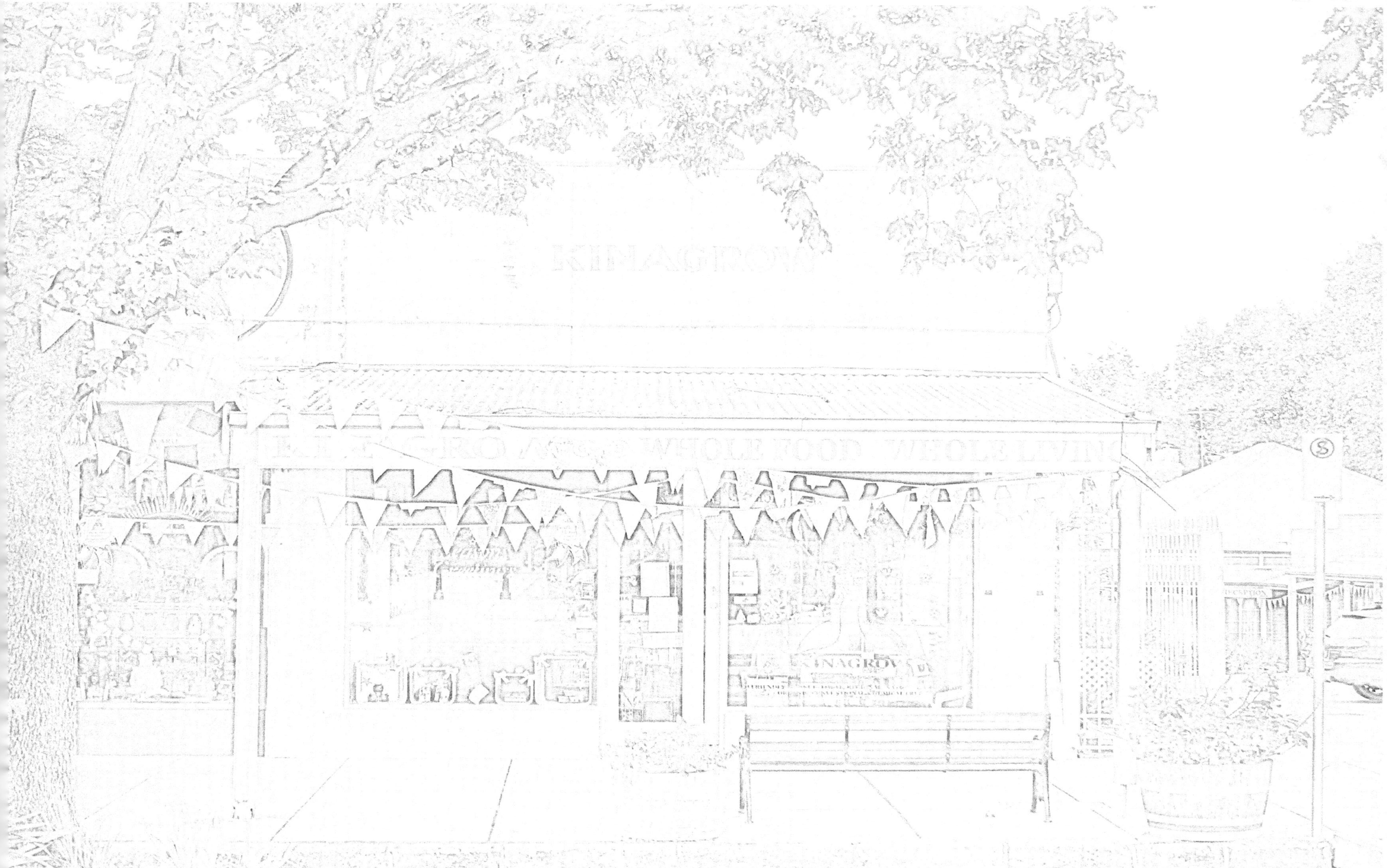
KINAGROW
WHOLE FOOD WHOLE LIVING
KINAGROW

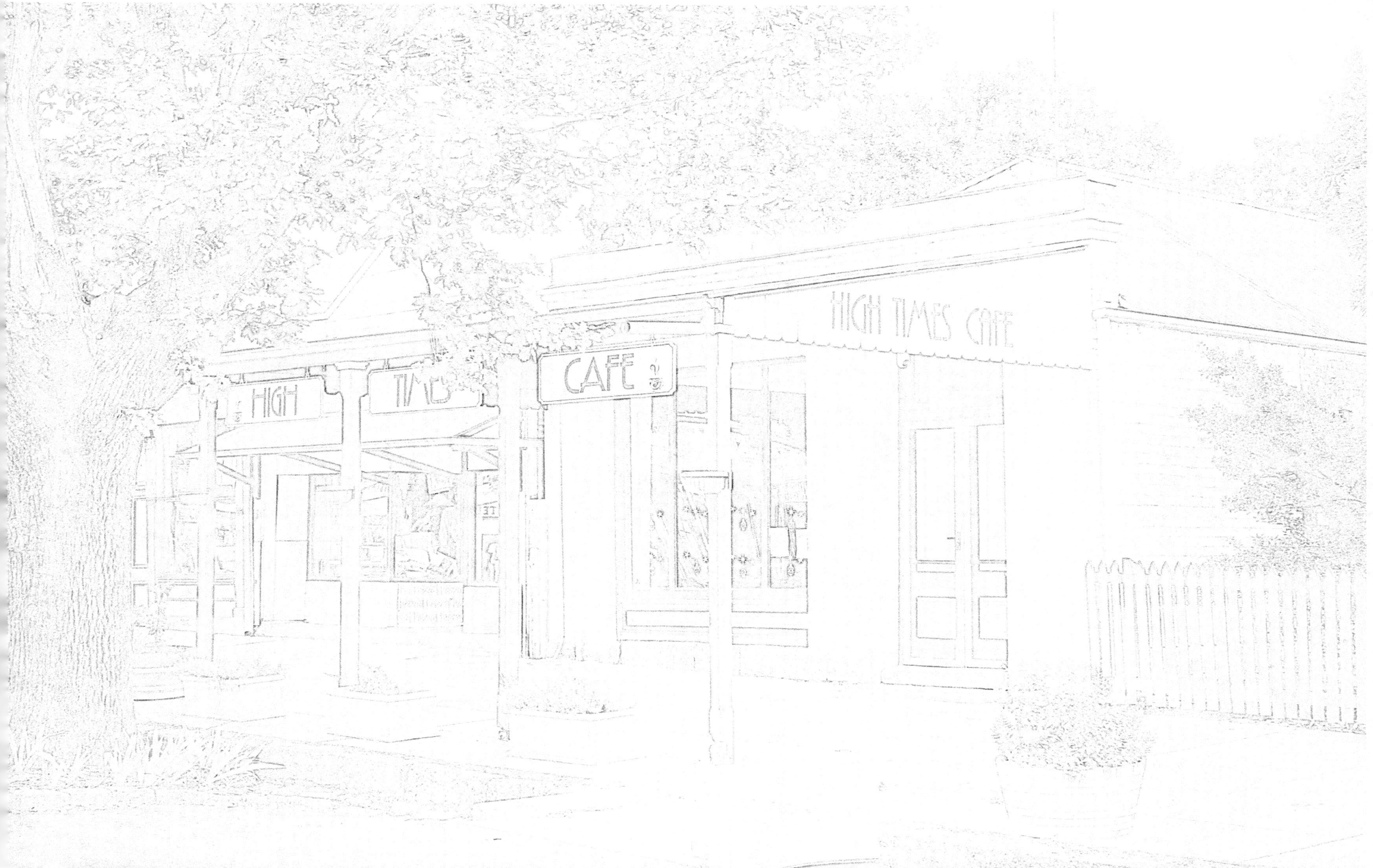
HIGH TIMES CAFE
CAFE
HIGH

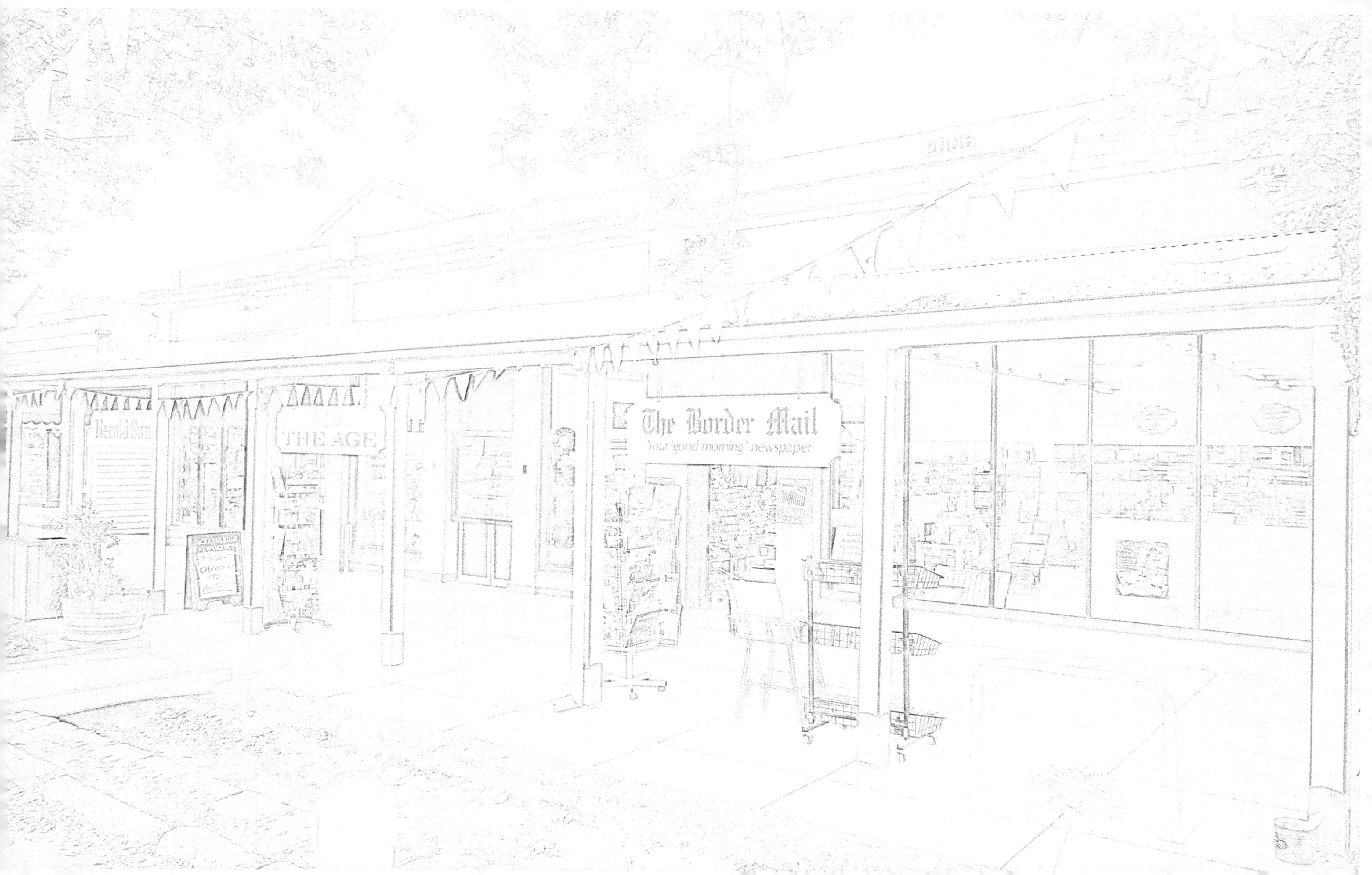

2006
Herald Sun
THE AGE
The Border Mail
Your 'good morning' newspaper

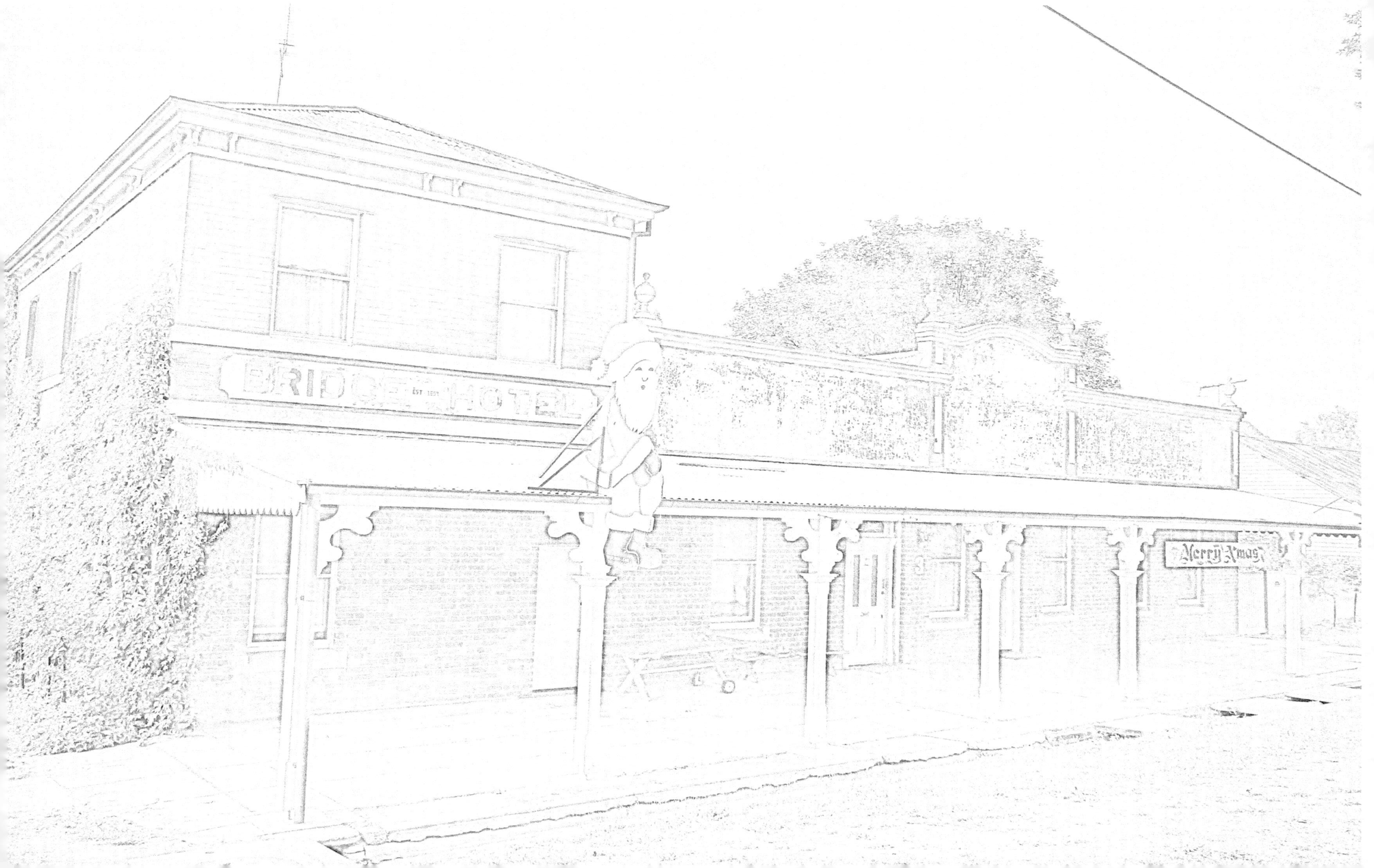
BRIDGE HOTEL
Merry Xmas

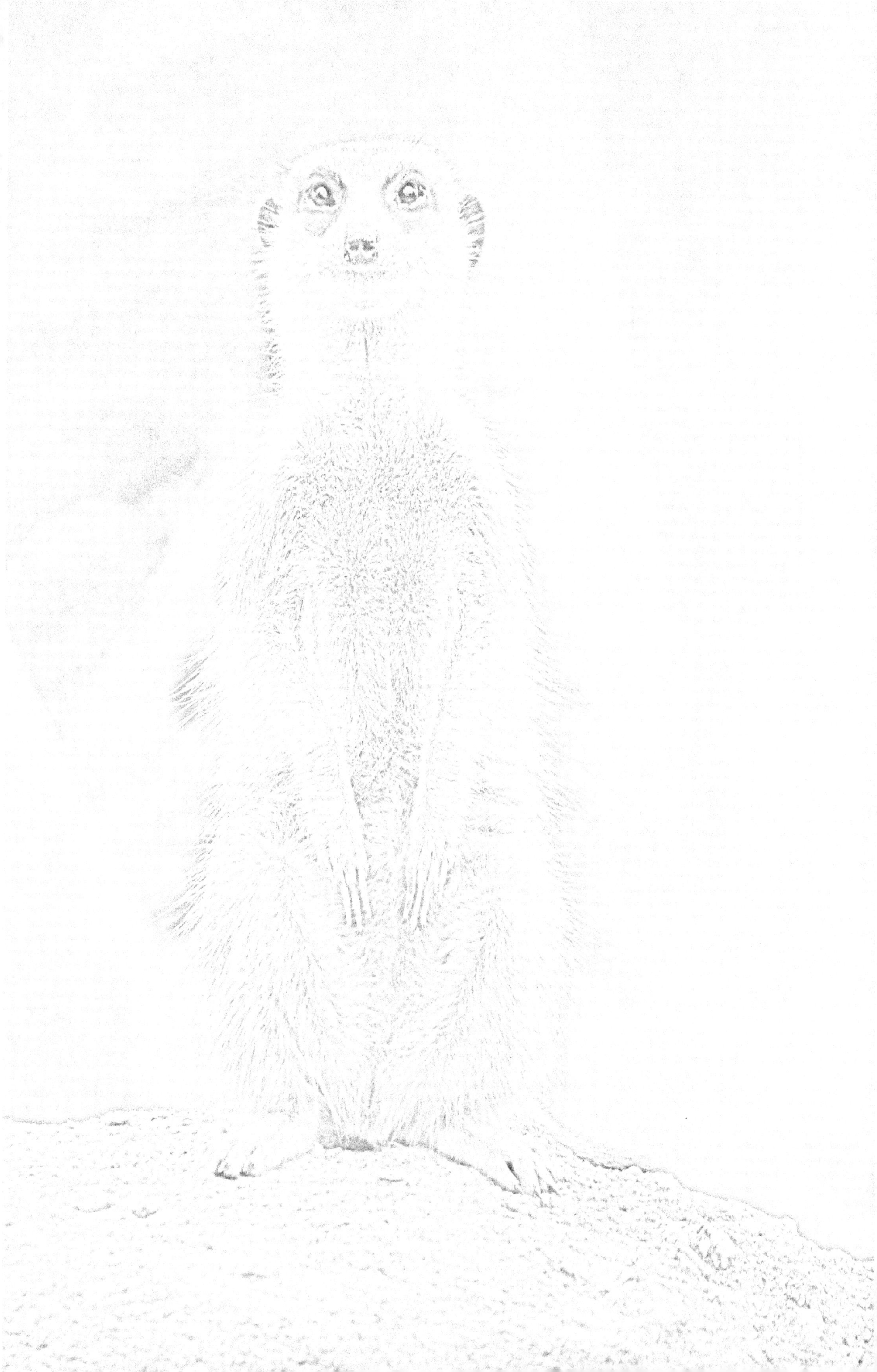

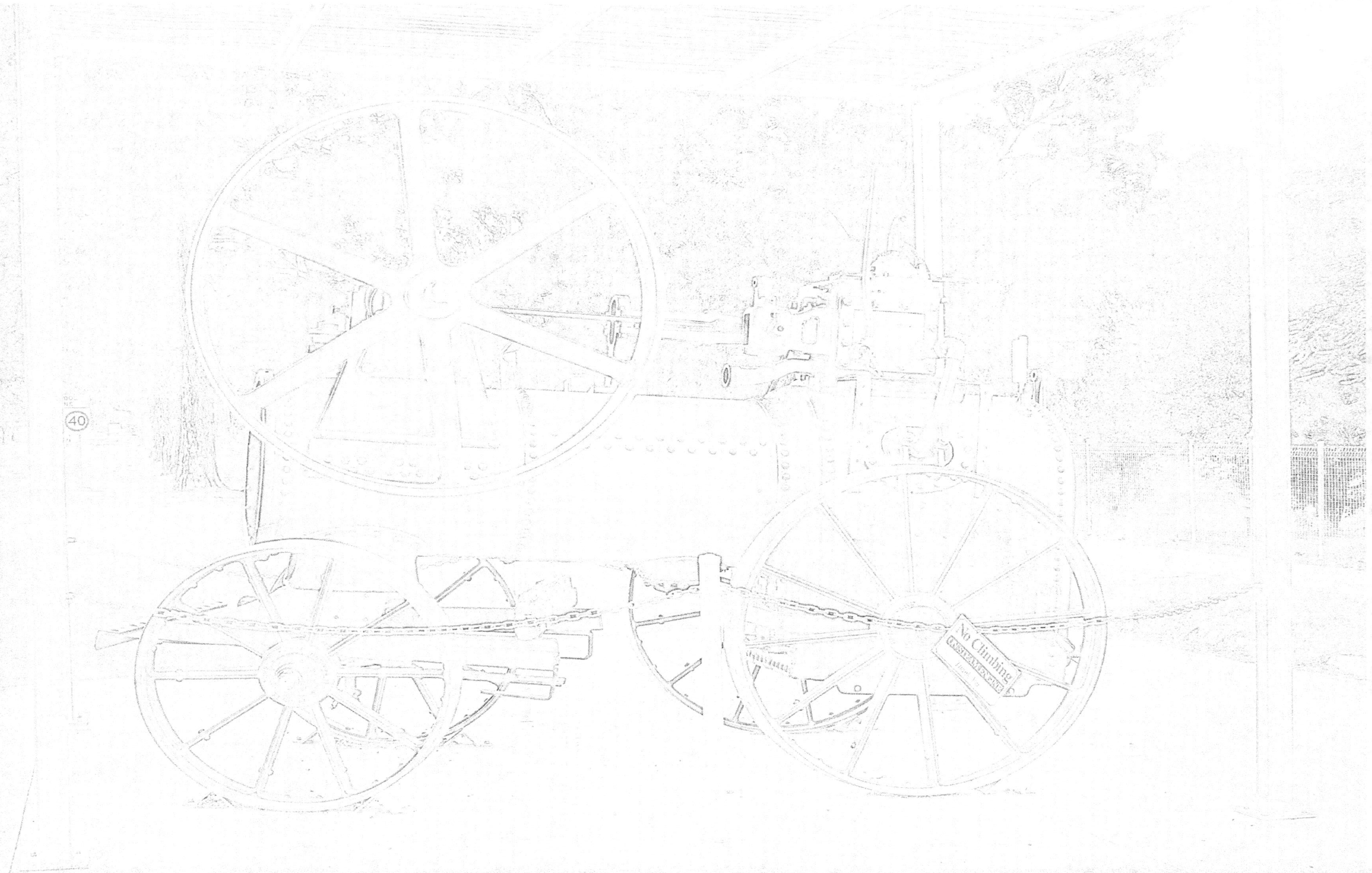
40
No Climbing

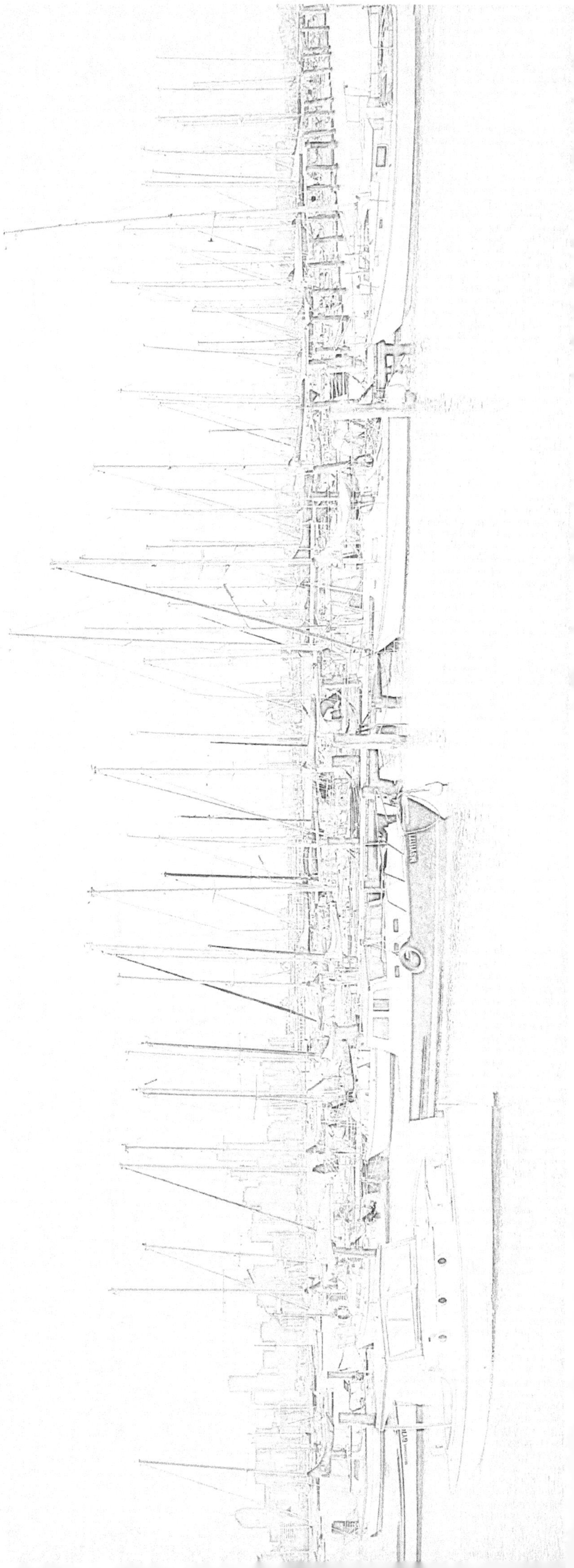

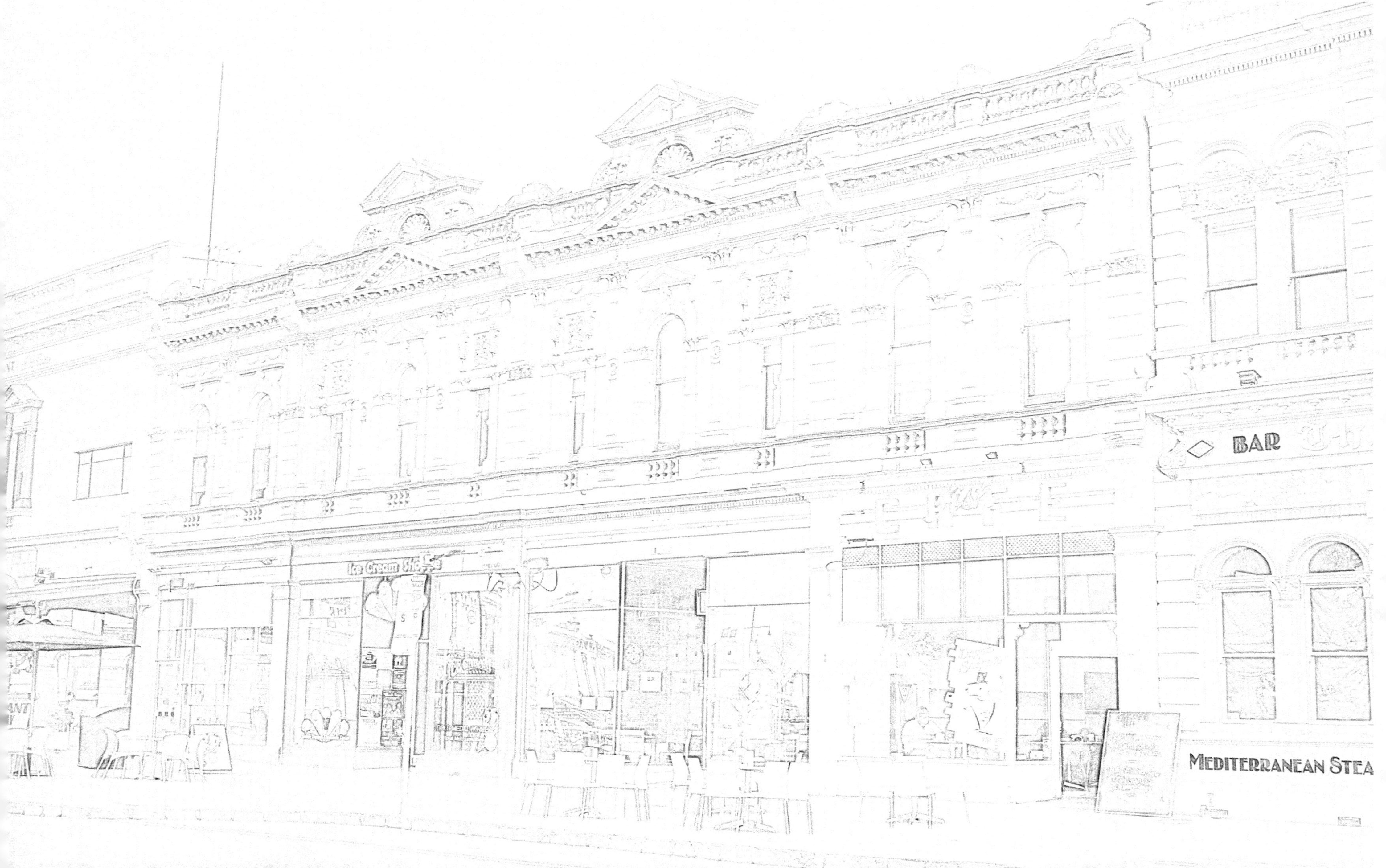
BAR
Ice Cream Sho
MEDITERRANEAN STEA

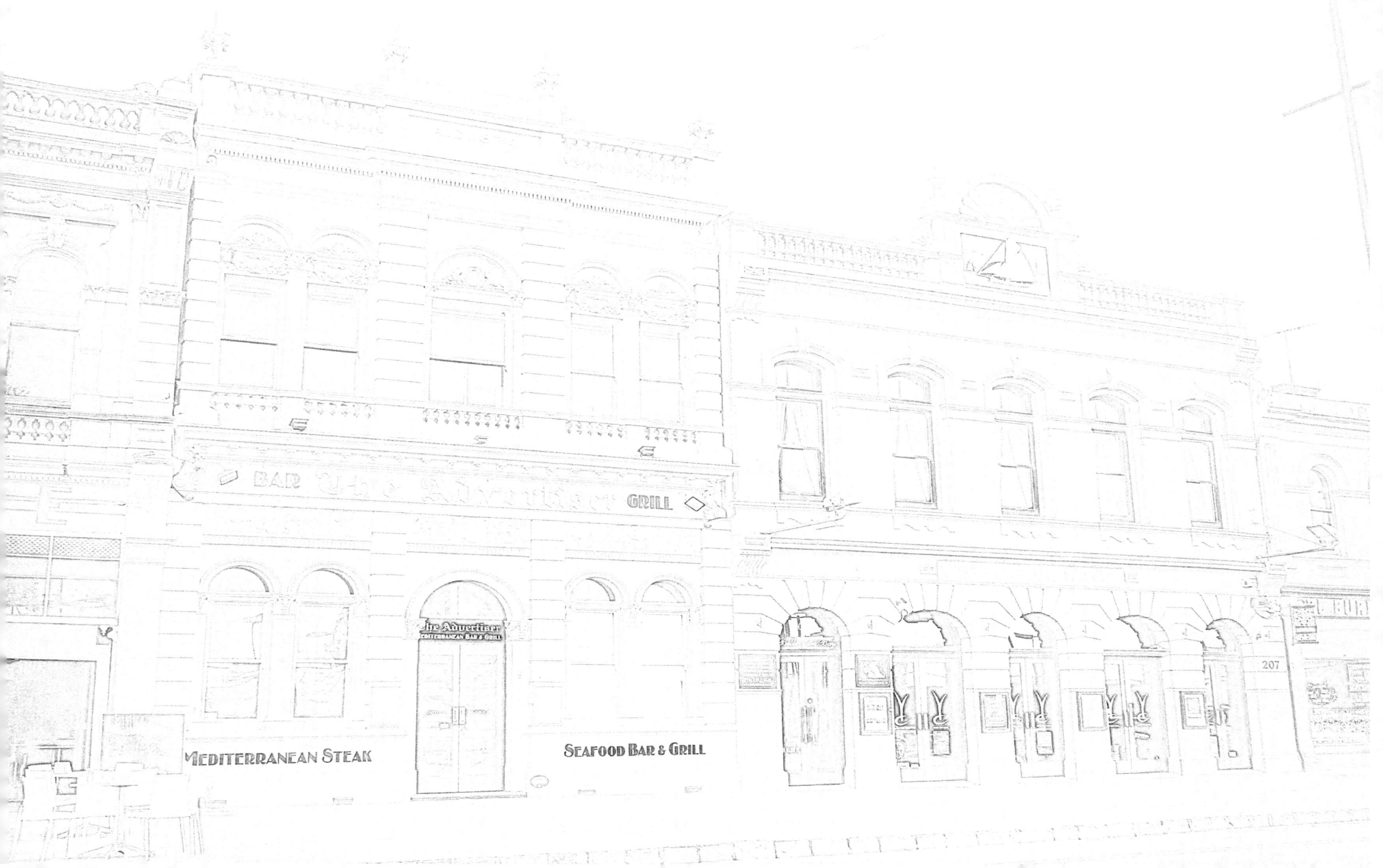
BAR
GRILL
The Advertiser
MEDITERRANEAN BAR & GRILL
MEDITERRANEAN STEAK
SEAFOOD BAR & GRILL
207

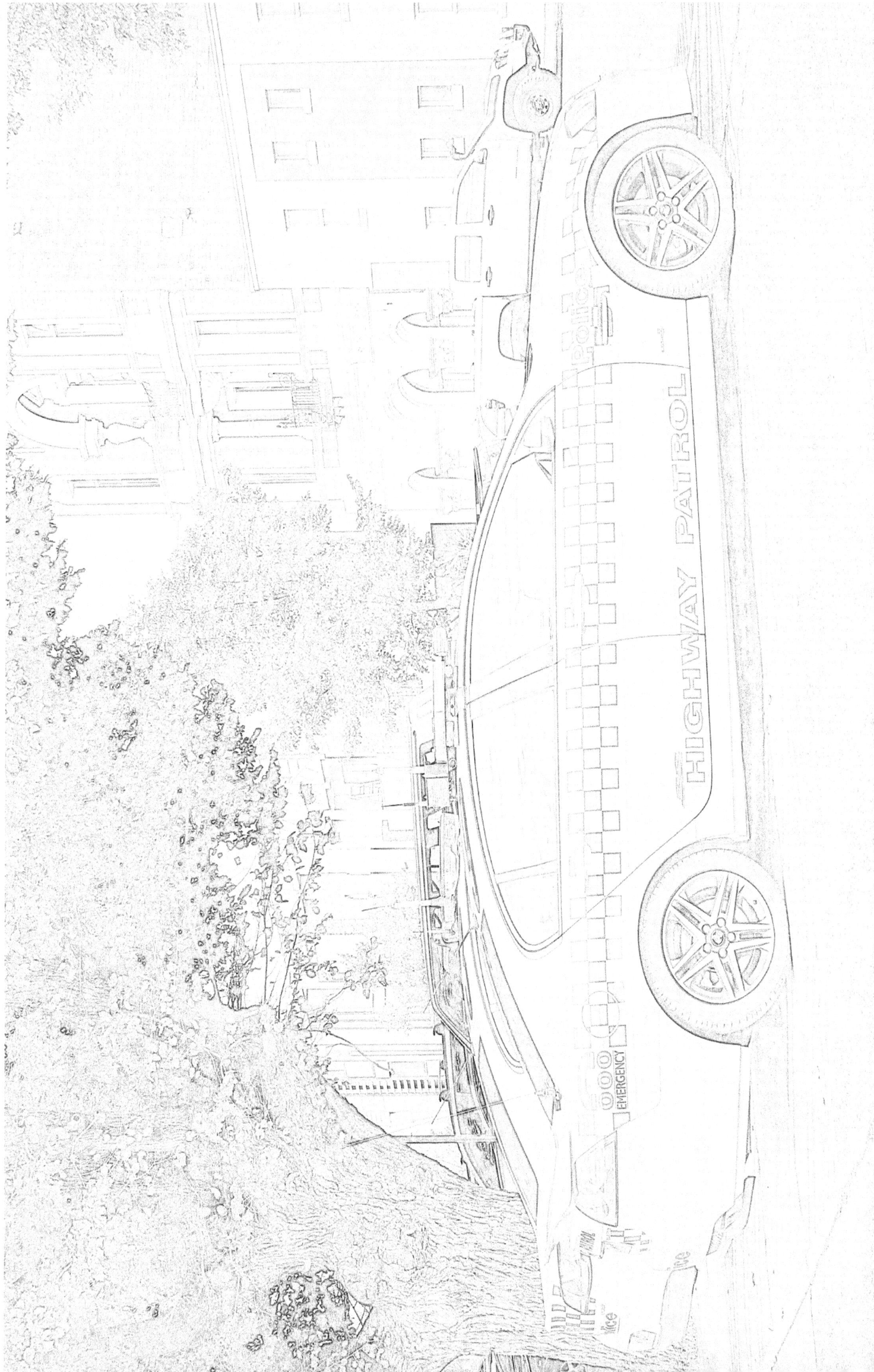
HIGHWAY PATROL
Police
000
EMERGENCY

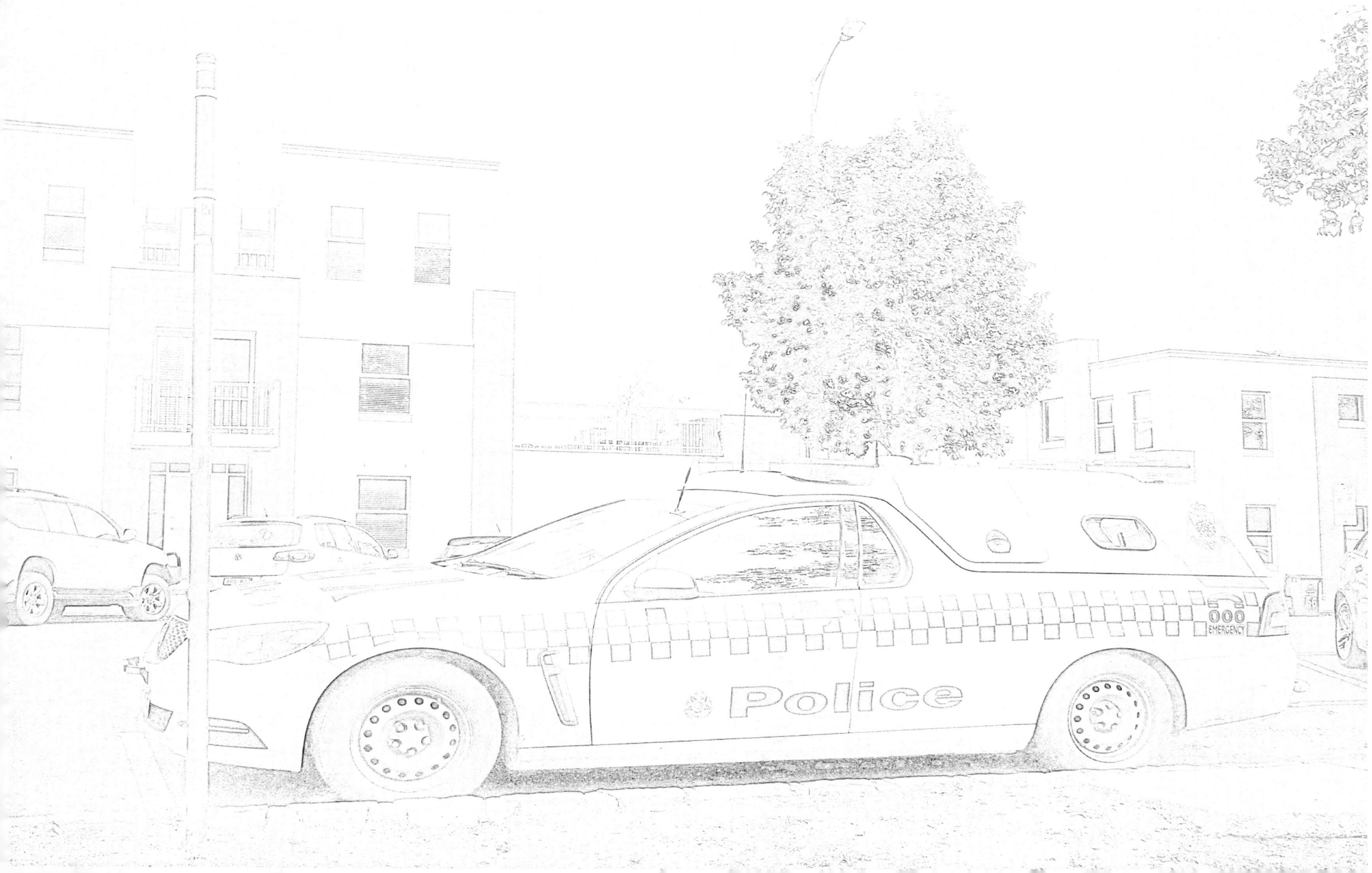
Police
000
EMERGENCY

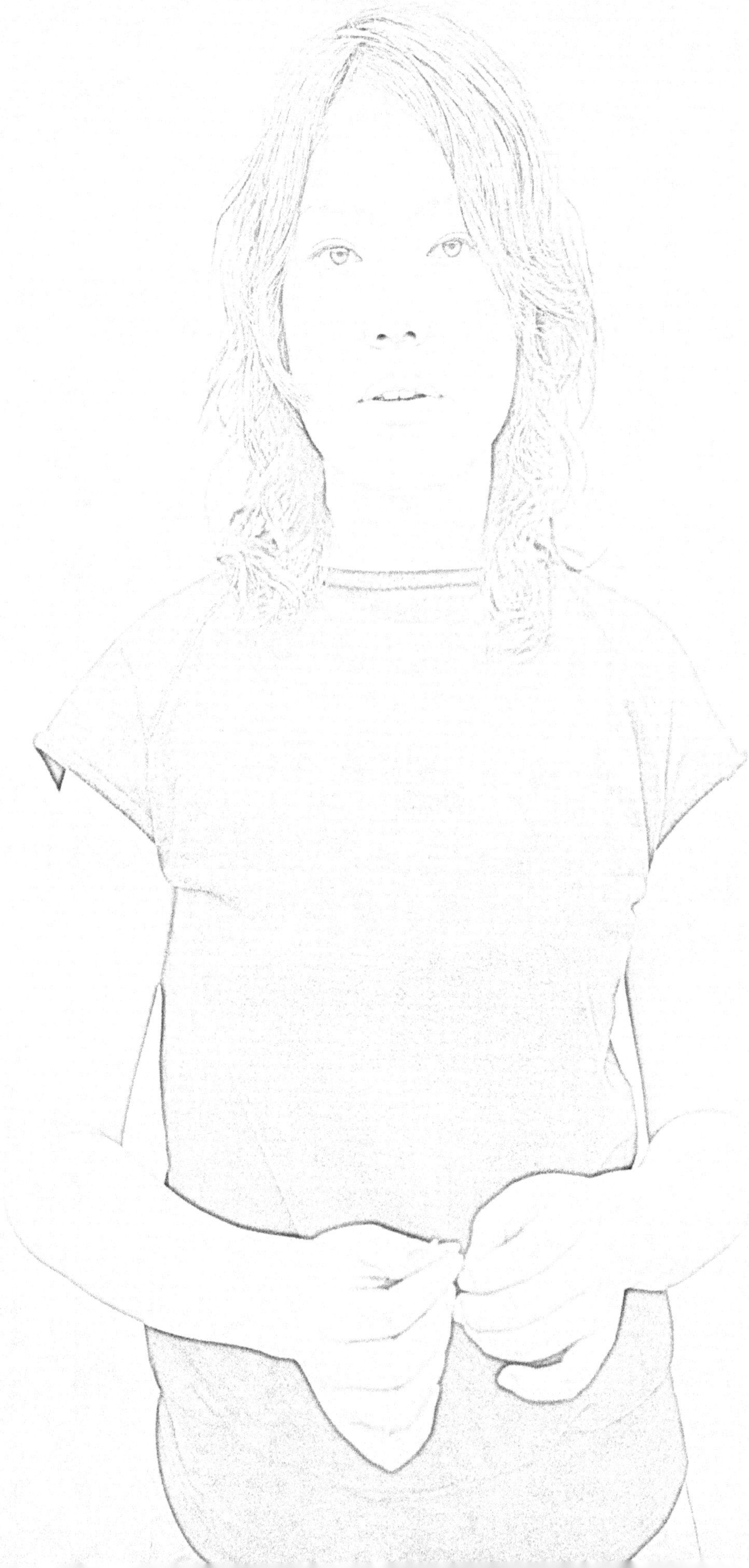

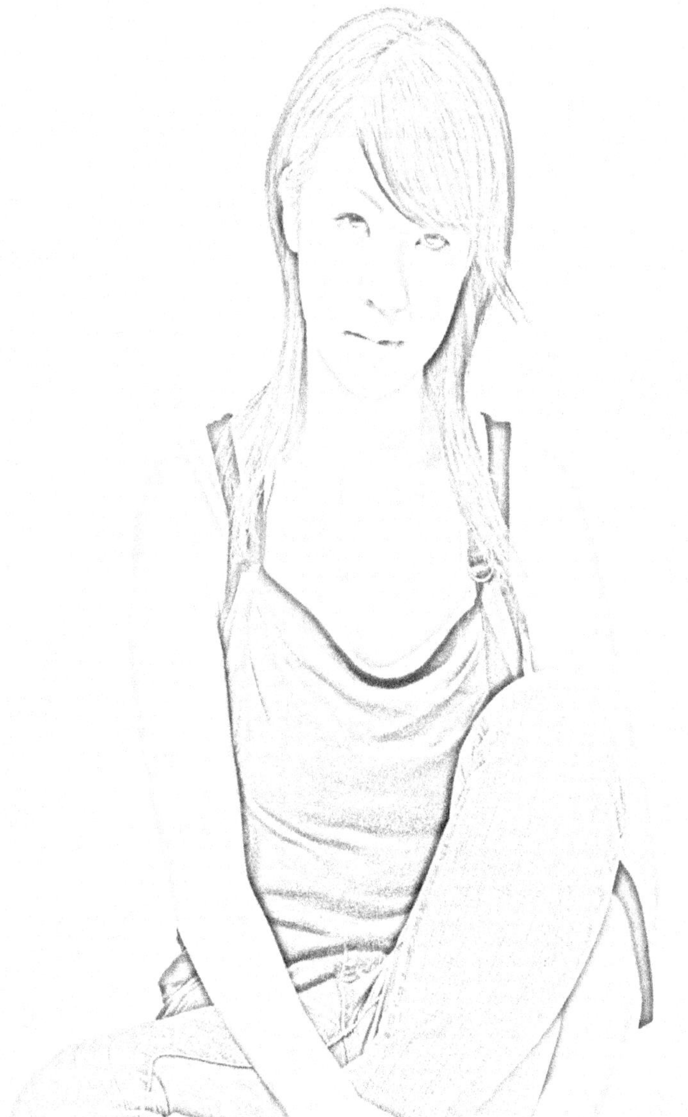

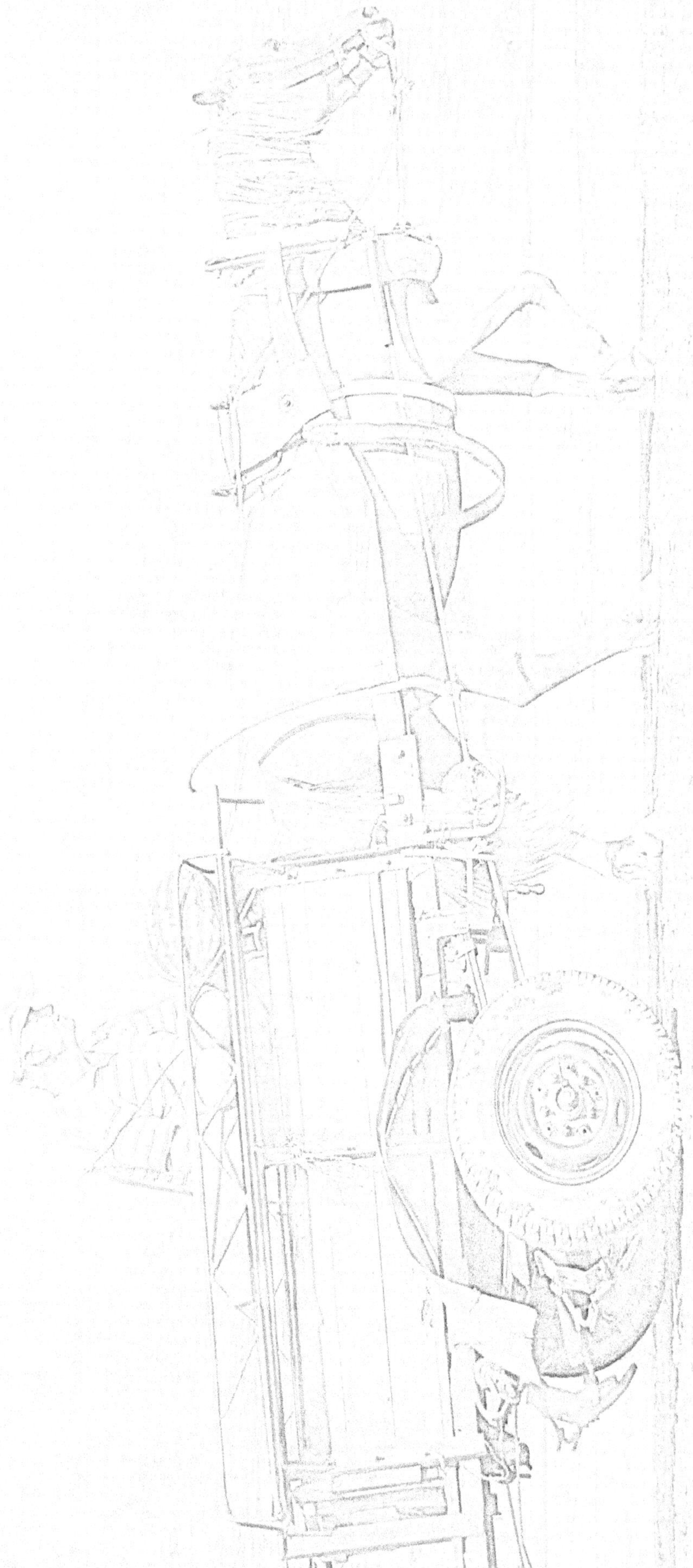

www.ingramcontent.com/pod-product-compliance
Lightning Source LLC
Chambersburg PA
CBHW081056180526
45170CB00005B/1783
* 9 7 8 0 3 5 9 8 6 3 4 0 2 *